Postmodern Canadian Fiction and the Rhetoric of Authority

Postmodern Canadian Fiction and the Rhetoric of Authority

GLENN DEER

McGill-Queen's University Press
Montreal & Kingston • London • Buffalo

© McGill-Queen's University Press 1994
ISBN 0-7735-1159-8
Legal deposit first quarter 1994
Bibliothèque nationale du Québec

Printed in Canada on acid-free paper

This book has been published with the help of a grant from the Canadian
Federation for the Humanities, using funds provided by the Social
Sciences and Humanities Research Council of Canada.

Chapter 2 of this study appeared as "Miracle, Mystery and Authority:
ReReading *The Double Hook*," in *Open Letter*, ser. 6, no. 8 (Summer
1987). Revised versions of parts of chapters 1 and 6 have been published
as "The Politics of Modern Literary Innovation: A Rhetorical
Perspective," in *Dalhousie Review* 70 (Fall 1990), and an earlier version
of chapter 7 was published as "Rhetorical Strategies in *The
Handmaid's Tale*: Dystopia and the Paradoxes of Power," in *English Studies
in Canada* 18 (June 1992).

Canadian Cataloguing in Publication Data

Deer, Glenn
    Postmodern Canadian fiction and the rhetoric of authority
    Includes bibliographical references and index.
    ISBN 0-7735-1159-8
    1. Canadian fiction (English) – 20th century – History and criticism. 2.
    Postmodernism (Literature) – Canada. I. Title.
    PS8199.D44 1994   C813'.5409   C93-090596-2
    PR9199.5D44 1994

This book was typeset by Typo Litho Composition Inc. in 10/12 Palatino.

Contents

Acknowledgments

This study is a substantially revised version of a doctoral dissertation I completed at York University, and I would like to express my deep thanks to those who provided critical feedback on my work as it evolved: I am particularly indebted to Frank Davey, who encouraged me to take critical risks and who supported the project with much wisdom and generosity. Many thanks are also due to Linda Hutcheon and Ian Sowton for their suggestions, to Robert Cluett and to the late Eli Mandel for guidance, and to the anonymous reviewers of the Canadian Federation for the Humanities, who provided critical comments that were most helpful in the improvement and rewriting of the manuscript. I wish to thank in particular Susan Kent Davidson at McGill-Queen's, whose expert editorial advice greatly enhanced this work. I would also like to thank my wife, Fay Ferris, for critical feedback and unlimited support.

Postmodern Canadian Fiction and the Rhetoric of Authority

1 Rhetorical Interventions and Literary Politics

Even as Aristotle is teaching one man how most effectively to make people say "yes," he is teaching an opponent how to make them say just as forceful a "no."

Kenneth Burke, *A Rhetoric of Motives*

The self of the orator is also an interpretation mediated by codes ... The self is always written, always interpreted, always "rhetorical."

George Dillon, Prologue, *Rhetoric as Social Imagination*

RHETORICAL INTERVENTIONS: A PRELUDE

There was a time when rhetoric was thought of as something that a classical orator studied to be an effective communicator, to project a persuasive presence, or to construct a compelling ethos through the employment of figurative devices. Literary rhetoric has often been mistakenly characterized as an ingredient that might simply be added to one's discourse, like additional spice to a verbal brew. Indeed, rhetoric has often had its fierce detractors: in Plato's *Gorgias* Socrates accuses the Sophists of teaching a form of mere cookery, a "knack of producing gratification and pleasure" (23). This reduction of rhetoric to a supplemental and ingratiating ingredient has also been exemplified in some very traditional and conservative works of literary rhetorical criticism, like Brian Vickers' *Classical Rhetoric and English Poetry* (1970), which have focused almost entirely on describing the deployment of tropes and schemes. But this style-centred approach has been outdated for some time. Modern rhetorical theorists with a special interest in literary interpretation have in various ways rehabilitated and revitalized classical rhetorical precepts and refreshed our understanding of the interactive contexts and rhetorical dimensions of literary experience. This is apparent in the early work of Kenneth Burke on agonism, or social competition and hierarchy, in *A Rhetoric of Motives* (1950), in the persistent attention to authorial stances and implied belief-systems in Wayne Booth's *The Rhetoric of Fiction* (1961) and *The Company We Keep* (1988), and in the recent pragmatic hermeneutics of Stephen Mailloux's *Rhetorical Power* (1989) or the social-interaction work of George Dillon's *Rhetoric as Social Imagination* (1986). Along with numerous communication theorists, speech-act theorists, rhetoricians, reader-response critics, compositionists, cultural theorists, social constructionists, and post-structuralists, critics like Dillon and Burke participate in what has been called the rhetorical turn in twentieth-century thought.

Modern rhetorical theory sees the critical practice of reading as a transactional activity in which authorial performances are not simply objectively described but recovered through an ideologically interested act of interpretation. As Dick Leith and George Myerson emphasize in *The Power of Address* (1989),"underlying Rhetoric ... is a sense of perpetual dialogue between speakers and listeners (who in turn can also speak), proposition and counter proposition, question and answer. Any assertion promotes or inspires an alternative or opposed formulation" (3).

There is a key passage in Kenneth Burke's *Philosophy of Literary Form* (1973) that has influenced many modern rhetorical theorists, including Stephen Mailloux (see *Rhetorical Power* 58); the metaphor that Burke provides therein is also central to the kind of rhetorical intervention into the site of Canadian literature that this book attempts to launch. Burke offers us the following "fable":

Imagine that you enter a parlor. You come late. When you arrive, others have long preceded you, and they are engaged in a heated discussion, a discussion too heated for them to pause and tell you exactly what it is about. In fact, the discussion had already begun long before any of them got there, so that no one present is qualified to retrace for you all the steps that had gone before. You listen for a while, until you decide that you have caught the tenor of the argument; then you put in your oar. Someone answers; you answer him; another comes to your defense; another aligns himself against you, to either the embarrassment or gratification of your opponent, depending upon the quality of your ally's assistance. However, the discussion is interminable. The hour grows late, you must depart. And you do depart, with the discussion still vigorously in progress. (*Philosophy* 111)

Burke's description of the "unending conversation" is an allegory of how we enter into the communities of human discourse that surround us. It is a particularly appropriate and enabling model of critical and rhetorical activity. Imagine entering the critical parlour of Canadian literature at different points in time. In the 1960s and early 1970s the popular, commanding, and authoritative presences holding forth in this parlour would include Northrop Frye, Eli Mandel, Margaret Atwood, George Woodcock, and many others with a special interest in thematic analysis of archetypal patterns and national mythology. In the 1970s and 1980s discussion in the parlour would be joined by a more contentious and oppositional group, proponents of a critical view that argued with other critical views and sought to shift away from thematic readings and towards the closer analysis of language, especially the formal innovations that have characterized the Canadian avant garde – in, for instance, the early work of Frank Davey, George Bowering, and Robert Kroetsch. And in the 1990s, what was once seen as marginalized, or subversive of the norm, has now become a new and highly respected standard: the pluralism, heterogeneity, and playfulness of the postmodernist perspective, and the politically sophisticated criticism of cultural semioticians like Linda Hutcheon, Frank Davey, Arthur Kroker, and many others.

Hence, for the student and critic of Canadian literature, disagreement and debate have been part of the history of our critical parlour. We have learned how to participate in the discussions that form our Canadian and postmodern literary, social, and political attitudes by studying the past and present idioms of specific critical domains, by taking sides on issues, and by responding to imaginary or real allies and opponents, or interlocutors. As we participate, we learn to adjust, modify, and develop critical and rhetorical strategies that will influence our fellow literary critics. This ongoing conversation might be dominated by certain paradigms – for example, the paradigms of literary romanticism, the New Criticism, formalism, myth criticism, psychoanalytic theory, Marxism, deconstruction, or feminism – and particular privileged ways of thinking and speaking, or preferred topics, authorities, rules for proceeding, and rituals. As we participate in the unending critical conversations – say, taking up our opponents' New Critical reading of a modernist poem by Irving Layton, or objecting to a patriarchally biased reading of myth and archetype in the novels of Robert Kroetsch and Leonard Cohen – we put in our oars and attempt to steer the discussion in a different direction. We accept the judgments of our perceived allies and we resist the positions of others. And we are constantly aware of the power-plays and authority of the positions that have the greatest influence in our readings.

Reading, of course, might be accompanied by a self-conscious attitude of resistance. Consider this passage from David Bartholomae and Anthony Petrosky's *Ways of Reading* as a model for a resistant rhetorical reception:

Reading involves a fair measure of push and shove. You make your mark on a book and it makes its mark on you. Reading is not simply a matter of hanging back and waiting for a piece, or its author, to tell you what the writing has to say. In fact, one of the difficult things about reading is that the pages before you will begin to speak only when the authors are silent and you begin to speak in their place, sometimes for them – doing their work, continuing their projects – and sometimes for yourself, following your own agenda ... We think of reading as a social interaction – sometimes peaceful and polite, and sometimes not so peaceful and polite. (1)

All of us play our roles in rhetorical exchanges by being the audience for the sales pitches of advertisements, the campaign speeches of politicians, the editorial columns of newspaper pundits, a critic's review of a book by Margaret Atwood, or the opening enticements of a best-selling suspense novel. But we are never just the passive recipients of such pitches, speeches, columns, reviews, or story beginnings: this is the point of Bartholomae and Petrosky's model of reading. The ad writers, politicians, editorialists, reviewers, and novelists who seek to use the available means of persuasion – in Aristotle's sense, the ethical appeals (virtuous character), pathetic appeals (stirring the audience's emotions), and logical appeals (use of reasoned arguments) – do not always persuade us to accept their views, interpretations, or values. We push back when we mentally argue against the persuader, countering persuasion with scepticism or an ironic self-awareness of the position we are supposed to play but cannot succumb to. In such cases we may even create a counter-rhetoric, the beginning of a alternative critical movemment.

Writers themselves are often the resistant readers of the literary sites where they hope to intervene. Literary innovators often enter into an intertextual competition to deal with the influence of literary ancestors. To subvert the values of the past or to be heard in the ongoing cultural conversation, they can try to change the written rhetoric or denounce the authority, discursive practices, or rhetoric of past writers. This is essentially the argument that Harold Bloom presents in *The Anxiety of Influence*, although in a somewhat patriarchal and nostalgic tone: strong writers who are highly conscious of their indebtedness to precursors will compete with canonical authors – "father" figures who can control the range of their "sons'" development – and struggle to establish an original imaginative space for their writing (5). Experiments in form are a necessary part of the rhetorical struggle to cope with the pressures of influence, to be original, and to establish a distinct identity.

To regard literary innovation as an intertextual power struggle accords with postmodern views of the centrality of power in discourse and social relations. Michel Foucault has stated that "the history which bears and determines us has the form of a war" (*Power/Knowledge* 114), and Linda Hutcheon says "we owe to Roland Barthes the strong formulation if not the concept that language is always fascist and that power is involved in even the most subtle mechanisms of social exchange" (*Canadian Postmodern* 74). Discourses of power and the filiations of authority in social relations are central to contemporary theories of experimental writing. This book explores these first by presenting an overview of the power politics of literary innovation, especially postmodern innovation. I believe that rhetorical interventions into postmodern writing are necessary in order to understand more fully the claims of postmodern innovation, and the methods of rhetorical interventions in the work of Roger Fowler and George Dillon will later be examined. Subsequent chapters will present rhetorically minded readings of important innovative Canadian novels. These readings will invite debate and controversy and enter in a practical way upon the project of imagining texts from a rhetorical perspective and supplementing the unending conversation that constitutes the site of the Canadian critical parlour.

THE POLITICS OF LITERARY INNOVATION

The works of avant-garde artists, including innovative or experimental novelists, do foster certain values, ways of seeing the world, or judgments concerning the way we should or should not live our lives. The ideological dimensions of texts have certainly been the focus of politically oriented critics working in many Marxist or feminist modes of inquiry. Roger Fowler reminds us that all literature is a form of social discourse, for "inescapably, a narrative text implies through its wording a narrating voice, the tone of an implicit speaker taking a line on his subject and adopting a stance towards his readers" (*Linguistics* 75). Experimental novelists cannot avoid constructing a stance towards their readers and promoting their concepts.

A close examination of theories of experimental writing, not surprisingly, reveals divided opinions on the importance of the political aspects of formal experiment, and complicates our attempts to describe the rhetorical strategies and concepts of authority in experimental practice. The social implications of innovation or experiment in the novel, and the experimenter's attitude to power and authority, must first be framed by the contexts of the sociology and philosophy of art. The very meaning of experimentalism, innovation, or the *idea* of the avant-garde in art has anti-authoritarian implications. As Renato Poggioli observes in *The Theory of the Avant-Garde,* the present experimental vanguard always becomes an institution against which future generations must argue and struggle in order to establish their own originality and novelty (80). The specific elements of any experimental art must be different from generation to generation, for it is originality and novelty that displace competitors from the locus of attention in the art world and allow the new art movement to dominate momentarily.

The history of the experimental novel is no exception to this process of competition, struggle, and generational conflict. In the nineteenth century, Zola opposed the subjective fantasies of "idealists" and "purely imaginary novels" (*Experimental Novel* 18); he defined the experimental novel as a scientific method of empirical observation, an approach to human behaviour that is literally an "experiment." Through his realistic naturalism he sought to reveal the biological and social causes of human action; he wanted the novel to be a tool for social and psychological analysis and argued that the novelist should be regarded as "an observer and an experimentalist [who] sets his characters going in a certain story so as to show that the succession of facts will be such as the requirements of the determinism of the phenomena under examination call for" (8).

In the early twentieth century, modernists like James Joyce, Virginia Woolf, and Dorothy Richardson – stylistically more innovative but less obviously political than the upcoming Orwells and Koestlers – evolved their own experiments for probing human reality. Their experiments with non-linear narrative and metaphorical renderings of psychological states can be seen as both a rejection of the demands of Zola's objective realism and a radical fulfilment of such demands. More recent experimenters in the novel, labelling themselves "postmodernists," "post-realists," and "fabulators" (see Klinkowitz, Federman, Scholes, and Stevick), continue the process of generational rebellion and assert that they are interested neither in the empirical investigations of naturalism nor in the phenomenological investigations of the psychological novelist: the contemporary experimental novelist is preoccupied with the writing process, with the conundrums of self-reflexive narrative, with the linguistic pattern of the text, and sometimes with the novel's gamelike features. John Hawkes writes of seeing "plot, character, setting, and theme" as "the true enemies" of the novel and of "having abandoned these familiar ways of thinking about fiction, totality of vision or structure was really all that remained" (quoted in Bradbury, *The Novel Today* 7). This recent, defensive emphasis on pure form and structure seems entirely at odds with the empirically motivated study of living characters and concrete environments that Zola saw as the novel's purpose in the nineteenth century.

Of course, formal self-awareness is not peculiar to contemporary experimental novels; it has been an aspect of the novel, as Malcolm Bradbury reminds us, since its emergence in the seventeenth and eighteenth centuries. And ever since its emergence, Bradbury says, the novel's two reputations have "both contested and consorted with each other": the "process of oscillation" between realism and fabulation that has been so marked in the twentieth century, that seems to distinguish the two sides of a current "debate" about the novel, is generated by two different impulses that have always been part of the nature of the novel. On the one hand there is "the novel's propensity toward realism, social documentation and interrelation with historical events and movements," and on the other there is "its propensity toward form, fictionality and reflexive self-examination"(Bradbury 8). In the nineteenth century it was the extreme swing to the former that was an innovative, experimental, or radical gesture; in the twentieth century, it is the swing to the latter.

Since the late nineteenth century, thus, the elements constituting an experimental novel have changed along with the evolving interests of different generations. The present generation of post-war experimental novelists are hostile to scientific empiricism, condescending to the conventions of realism, and distrustful of political conservatism, or indeed, distrustful of politics in general. Having inherited a romantic contempt for classical notions of imitation, as Poggioli suggests, the only "constants" that modern experimental art will readily admit to being bound to are restlessness, discontent with the past, and a hostility to "conservative" authority, beliefs, values, and conventions (*Theory of the Avant Garde* 80).

All literature, whether one emphasizes its tendency towards realism or its inclination towards anti-mimetic lexical play, presents world-views or ideologies, and, often, critical attitudes to particular social institutions, to the use of power, and to the nature of particular forms of authority. However, the contemporary experimental novel is often more emphatic in its promotion of counter-ideology. Distinctly different from realism in its formal preoccupations, it often presents radical philosophical and political concepts, is preoccupied with

power and authority, and a revolutionary or counter-ideological political status is claimed for it by many of its partisan critics or the novelists themselves – even if this political status is sometimes one that
denies that ideological and political views are a part of the novelist's
interests.

Among those theorists who promote experimental writing, there
are three views of the relationship between literature and politics: one
response is to argue that the experimental techniques – discontinuous
forms, self-reflexivity, linguistic play, and anti-mimetic elements – are
truly revolutionary because they resist the oppressive homogeneity
that is enforced by the dominant institutions in modern society. A
second response is to contend that experimental technique is entirely
divorced from political or ideological interest and that writers do not
intend to sell the reader any political bill of goods, only the textually
enclosed experience of reading a novel. A third response is to argue
that experimental writing presents paradoxical political positions that
both affirm and undermine the status quo. Theorists who argue the
latter often emphasize the liberatory experience of aesthetic form and
downplay the rhetorical stance that the writer adopts towards the
reader. They hold that readers are free to construct their own experiences through the open-ended or paradoxical forms employed by the
author.

Herbert Marcuse represents the first type of theorist, the advocate
of experiment as cultural criticism. In *The Aesthetic Dimension*
Marcuse says that "the radical potential of art lies precisely in its ideological character," though "ideology is not always *mere* ideology, false
consciousness" (13) but signifies various types of belief, and degrees
of self-consciousness or perhaps self-delusion. He emphasizes that,
"as ideology, [art] opposes the given society. The autonomy of art
contains the categorical imperative: 'things must change'" (13). From
this general premise regarding the counter-ideological role of art in
society, Marcuse moves to explanations of how particular aesthetic
tactics are politically significant: "Discontinuous forms and fragmen-
tation are aesthetic *resistances* to the role and power of 'the whole'; of
the administered unification of man which saps his subjectivity – collage and multi-media effects are *not* a reflection of reality but a resistance to homogeneity" (50). Implicit in Marcuse's statement is a theory
of the oppressive authority of social institutions, which threatens individuality, subjectivity, and personal choice, and a belief that discontinuous forms offer one way of resisting such oppression in the realm
of literary experience.

It is important to note that Marcuse's theory, in which the values of
individuality, subjectivity, and personal freedom are equated with

non-linear, disrupted aesthetic forms, is similar to the theories connecting open form to liberal politics that were advanced by Canadian defenders of radical experiments in art in the inaugural 1970s period of Canadian postmodernism. This defence of disordering and polyphony is especially apparent in the early critical statements of Frank Davey, George Bowering, and Robert Kroetsch.

Though Davey and Bowering are both lively polemicists for postmodernism, they have different views of the political significance of formal experiment. Davey's position is similar to that of Marcuse, although Davey has carefully criticized and revised his initial theorizing about contemporary Canadian writing over the past twenty years: his current position is highly conscious of his own ideological positioning within critical debates in Canada (see especially *Reading Canadian Reading*, 1988). Bowering is more distrustful of ideological systems in general and emphasizes the playful dimensions of experimental forms. In Davey's early 1972 "guidebook" to contemporary Canadian literature, *From There to Here* – a work that deliberately parodies the authority of encyclopaedic survey texts – he writes that "the technical experiments of nichol, Coleman, Marlatt, and Matt Cohen are ultimately more revolutionary than the nationalism of Lee and Atwood" (22). Davey has consistently been politically committed to a decentralization of authority and a pluralistic society in which all individuals have access to communications and information technologies, but none has epistemological primacy over the others. In his later critical view as well, postmodernism is aligned with "the politics of region, semiotics, phenomenology, [and] open form" (*Reading* 41); it presents an alternative to the authority of a totalizing modernist humanism. The positivist world-view is attacked for being a distortion of the flux of existence. In his commentary on Gerry Gilbert's poetry, which he praises for being authentically postmodern, Davey defends the poet's deliberate avoidance of well-made form, for "neatness, conciseness, or rhetorical form would directly betray the randomness of reality he seeks to evoke, and merely duplicates the various institutional and political structures which he believes to distort life and oppress men"(*From There to Here* 119).

Epistemological distortion and authoritarian oppression are two concepts that are central to Davey's agonistic postmodernism: these are tyrannical forces that must be resisted, and they can be partly resisted by postmodern forms, which are both more honest or authentic and more free or democratic.

Davey's attitude to modernist philosophies of knowledge is comparable to that of Bowering, who appeals both more strongly and more paradoxically to the ethos of honesty and authenticity while de-

fending experimental fiction. For Bowering, being a post-realist experimental writer means greater formal self-consciousness (i.e., true
experimental professionalism), eschewal of realist illusionism, avoidance of naturalist assumptions of determinism, and an appreciation of
the pleasure of textual play. Bowering is playfully anti-ideological
and does not regard experimental writing as a direct form of political
intervention. He insists on the precise use of "experimental" to desig-
nate those writers who consciously manipulate conventions and deliberately play with or undermine the rules of genre: in his view, b.p.
Nichol is "a truly experimental writer" (Bowering, *Fiction* 15); however, Daphne Marlatt "is not an experimental writer ... but a phenomenological one, perhaps our most easily observable example of
Olson's proprioceptive writer" (14). For Bowering, traditional realist
fiction attempts to operate in a wholly referential fashion and de-
pends on "one's closing one's eyes to the facts" (*The Mask* 121) of form
(the frame of the theatrical stage), and the lexical surface of the text.
Realist fiction attempts to "produce a window on the world," and
hence such fiction values "invisibility" and "transparency," like the
Jamesian novel that never draws attention to itself as an artefact; but
postmodern novels are like "stained-glass windows or cut-glass windows that divert light waves and restructure the world outside" (25).
Bowering's emphasis on the non-representational, anti-mimetic function of postmodern writing is exemplified in his reference to the
American novelist Ronald Sukenick's comparison of contemporary
fiction to abstract painting: "You cannot look through it to reality – it
is the reality in question and if you don't see it you don't see anything
at all" (121).

But Bowering's example can lead to an unfortunate discounting of
the content, ideas, and representations of language. An eagerness to
praise the anti-referential forms and tactile surface pleasures and in-
trigues of postmodern fiction is ironically cast in metaphors like the
"stained-glass window."

Unlike Davey's theory, Bowering's defence of the new fiction does
not attempt to present any argument for relating anti-referentiality to
an ideology of anti-centrism or anti-authority. Instead, Bowering remains the playful sceptic, especially regarding the ability of writers to
capture social reality. Sometimes he equates realism with dogmatic
scientific determinism; the social analysis undertaken by the realist is,
in Bowering's view, as reductive as primitive psychoanalysis: "The
realist says what the Freudian analyst said, that behavior is explain-
able in terms of cause and effect, the relationship between individual
and society" (*The Mask* 80).The realist's means of achieving verisimil-
itude – textual evidence, motivated character, continuity of phenom-

ena – are presented as deceitful by Bowering: in fact Bowering is showing a form of rhetorical scepticism towards the artificial conventions of realist fictions: he is being a resistant reader. However, there are other instances in Bowering's theory where the argumentative dimension of fiction itself is seen as not rhetorically interested, as transparent, or as simply a form of reporting, for in his view, "a major function of the novel was always to bring the news, to tell the story of the emerging middle class, to document the ways of Black Americans, to report the doings of a homicide detective in Don Mills." According to Bowering, the depiction of our daily social reality was once best undertaken by the novel, "the clearest way to show the quotidian details of life in Bombay or Quebec"; now, however, "the sociology books and television can give us all the news we need" (*The Mask* 124).

For all of Bowering's consciousness of how form rhetorically affects our perceptual experience and cognition of the perceived object, he has, surprisingly, a "realist's" faith in the transparency of the "windows" of "sociology books and television." For if sociology books and television do shape our apprehension of the world – give us the news, so to speak – then we should understand how these forms influence, engage, or even manipulate our understanding of content. We should take a rhetorically sensitive approach to these potentially manipulative forms of communication.

Bowering's defence of the formal pleasures of post-realist fiction is eventually turned into what Gerald Graff calls a visionary strategy of transcendence (*Literature* 13): since fiction is deceitful if it tries to convey the real world, then we will subsume the real world under the category of fiction and eliminate the problem of truthful representation. Thus, while the old realists "assumed that there was a real world one could make sense of and care enough about to want to correct," the present writers are less naïve; as Bowering states, "A lot of novelists will agree that the real world is a fiction, one of a number of them, from any logical or phenomenological viewpoint a fiction" (*The Mask* 126). One might assume that this casting of reality into fiction well serves Bowering's distrust of all ideologies and his anti-realism. But the notion that the world is a fictional construct actually supports our understanding of the world: to say that the world is a fiction implies that you do know something of importance about external reality – it is a construction, and perhaps a construction that can be understood, resisted, or even revised. If the external world is built up from fictions, or socially constructed knowledge, then we should attempt to understand what kinds of consciousness produce these fictions, how these fictions attempt to influence readers, and what kinds of world-views and social values are being promoted. Bowering's position has the unfortunate effect of presenting experimental fictions as ideologically innocent, as using ideas that do not originate in human political interests and forms that are not rhetorically designed to promote the assimilation of particular beliefs and values.

Brian McHale, in his *Postmodernist Fiction*, holds that the contemporary novel is "above all an illusion-breaking art; it systematically disturbs the air of reality by foregrounding the ontological structure of texts and of fictional worlds" (221). Linda Hutcheon also praises the subversive and critical potential of postmodern art in her *Politics of Postmodernism*, for "postmodernism works to 'de-doxify' [denormalize] our cultural representations and their undeniable political import" (3); yet Hutcheon also carefully qualifies the subversive power, for, as she emphasizes throughout her study, "[postmodern fiction] is a strange kind of critique, one bound up, too, with its own *complicity* with power and domination, one that acknowledges that it cannot escape implication in that which it nevertheless still wants to analyze and maybe even undermine" (4).

Many of the theorists who defend experimental fiction present contradictory attitudes towards writing and the real world and towards the relationship between novels and politics. As Gerald Graff has pointed out, they both attempt to withdraw from the world of politics and to swallow it (*Literature* 17). Robert Kroetsch, a witty and satirical spokesman for postmodern Canadian fiction, has said in an interview that he is "quite aware of being without ideology"; yet on the same occasion he remarked that he has a "very strong identification with that notion of a non-violent anarchy [represented in Bakhtin's revolutionary ideology of carnival] because all systems have been oppressive to us on the prairies" (*Labyrinths* 33). Kroetsch, like Bowering, would have us believe that he is without any ideological commitments; but like Marcuse and Davey he seeks to be identified as part of a regional counter-ideology. In fact, all the theorists that we have considered so far – Marcuse, Davey, Bowering, Kroetsch – all support, even by the paradoxical position of being anti-ideological, the adversarial role of art, and therefore place experimental fiction in a resistant and subversive role in society.

However, the political claims of experimental fiction – the equating of such elements as discontinuous form, authorial self-reflexivity, and linguistic play with liberal or revolutionary politics, or ideas that are opposed to reactionary or conservative values – have been scrutinized and criticized by Georg Lukács, Renato Poggioli, Fredric Jameson, Gerald Graff, and Charles Newman. All these critics test the political and epistemological claims made by experimental or avant-garde art.

Poggioli dismisses the political alignment of the avant-garde with revolutionary politics: "The identification of artistic revolution with the social revolution is now no more than purely rhetorical, an empty commonplace" (*Theory of the Avant-Garde* 96). Poggioli would seem to confirm Kroetsch's belief that experimental writing like Kroetsch's own is apolitical, for "the only omnipresent or recurring political ideology within the avant-garde is the least political or the most antipolitical of all: libertarianism and anarchism" (96). Lukács, in *The Meaning of Contemporary Realism*, opposes the celebration of solipsism and subjectivity in literature because such subjectivism merely multiplies the epistemological distortions that a capitalist society encourages in order to entrench its values; if literature is to be an authentic criticism of such a society, then "literature must have a concept of the normal if it is to 'place' distortion correctly; that is to say, to see it *as* distortion" (33). Lukács, in his aesthetic theory, has persistently criticized modern experimenters in fiction for being overly preoccupied with formal elements and technique to the neglect of ideas and emotions. His arguments for realism and truthful representation are posed in an even stronger way by Gerald Graff, who has been directly influenced by Lukács.

In his analyses of the politics of experimental art, Graff has tested the consistency of avant-garde ideology. First, he exposes the oversimplification and lack of sociological proof in avant-garde theories of authority and social repression, and he argues convincingly that postmodern counter-ideology, which celebrates its own alienation and marginality, is not really *counter* to the dominant ideology of the contemporary Western world, the ideology of advanced capitalism: the postmodern counter-ideology, ironically, is a symptom of advanced capitalism. Second, Graff carefully examines the arguments that relate the disrupted, anti-mimetic forms of literature to revolutionary politics, and he finds significant contradictions in these arguments.

In his essay "The Pseudo-Politics of Interpretation" Graff shows how radical interpretation theorists set up a quarrel with objective, rational critical theory: the radical relates objectivity to the ideology of modern authority, an authority that operates through structures of "centrism, hierarchy, and constraint" (in Mitchell, *Politics of Interpretation* 154). However, these depictions of how modern authority operates in the industrialized Western world, and the correspondences drawn between this authority and specific literary forms, are never supported by valid argument and proof. Commonplaces about technology and authority lead the radical theorist to purvey an outdated myth of the repressive nature of society. Liberation is not the panacea to our social woes, according to Graff, because it is not the strangling effect of social class that is the cause of postmodern malaise. An art that promotes revolution, non-linear flux, and is anti-ideological does not subvert the dominant ideology of the status quo but abets it. As Graff says, "the real avant-garde is advanced capitalism, with its built-in need to destroy all vestiges of tradition, all orthodox ideologies, all continuous and stable forms of reality in order to stimulate higher levels of consumption" (*Literature against Itself* 4).

We should note that Graff is not merely refuting the avant-garde's claim that it is resisting the authoritarian nature of social institutions. He is arguing that postmodernism – read experimentalism and avant-gardism – is in harmony with consumer sensibility, and hence it thrives. In our highly developed consumer society, discontinuities, perpetual changes in fashion, and ephemeral novelty have caused "a derangement of the senses that makes the disruptions and defamiliarizations of vanguard culture look puny by comparison" (*Literature against Itself* 92). Fredric Jameson has similarly described postmodern consumer culture as characterized by its lack of coherence and continuity as it encourages an appetite for "a perpetual change that obliterates traditions of the kind which all earlier social formations have had in one way or another to preserve" (in Kaplan, *Postmodernism* 28). As Graff says, "The juxtaposition of terror and triviality, consequence and irrelevance, in an average newspaper front-page or news broadcast does more to assault hierarchically ordered thinking than the most uncompromising example of anti-object art (*Literature against Itself* 97). John O'Neill also connects artistic experiment to the cultural fashions that drive contemporary consumer society when he states that "it is difficult to hang on to postmodernism's claim to be transgressive given the capacity of late capitalism to absorb and to neutralize every shock it imposes ... The faster the culture industry runs to outrage its bourgeoisie, the surer it can be of its own embourgeoisement" (in Silverman, *Postmodernism* 76).

In his analysis of the politics of the experimental, not only does Graff show that the epistemological scepticism of the anti-realist is contradictory – that is, to be able to recognize the unintelligibility of our "unreal" world *is* to propose a way of understanding the way things really are – but he also identifies the equivocation in modern intellectuals who attempt to eliminate the referential claims of art. Graff uses two aesthetic aphorisms from Oscar Wilde to exemplify the "formalist" and "visionary" strategies of anti-referential critics: on the one hand Wilde is a "formalist" who argues for the radical autonomy of the artefact, for "art never expresses anything but itself"; on the other, his aesthetic envelops the reality of the everyday world, and "life imitates art far more than art imitates life" (*Literature against*

Itself 18) – this is what Graff labels the "visionary" strategy. The formalist and visionary strategies reflect "the social ambivalence of the modern literary intellectual, who is tempted equally to withdraw from society and politics, and to try to take them over" (17). Both strategies are clearly subscribed to by George Bowering, who says that art "is the reality in question" and that the "real world is a fiction" (*The Mask* 124).

Graff defines some important theoretical problems in the arguments of critics who promote experimentalism. Borrowing from Graff, one can ask if experimental writers influence the reader's response through special rhetorical effects, disruptive forms, and narrative tactics that are part of a liberating mode of persuasion, and how the kinds of social authority they critique are specifically presented. In other words, one could describe the rhetorical tactics that authors use in their attempts to persuade readers to adopt certain positions, and to describe what understanding of authority the authors want the reader to have. For example, John Kuehl, in *Alternate Worlds*, claims that although "antirealistic fiction seems so rebellious and revolutionary," the cultural role assumed by the writers is conservative: "those appearing to be democratic are really autocratic" (298). Brian McHale also notes that the point of view of these writers is inherently manipulative, for "narratives 'seduce' their readers, in the sense that they solicit and attempt to manipulate relationships" (*Postmodernist Fiction* 222), and "the postmodernist author arrogates to himself the powers that gods have always claimed: omnipotence, omniscience" (210).

However, the pragmatic test of these claims about authorial power or rhetorical manipulation needs to be made through our imaginative engagement with the texts. We need to undertake what Graff does not: to describe how the experimental style affects the reader and to describe the specific social and political content or arguments presented in the novels. Graff concentrates his analysis on epistemology and the theory of discontinuous forms; but his critical practice lacks a rhetorical dimension. If we are to describe accurately how experimental novels either promote critical understanding of society or somehow disarm our intelligence, then we need to track the relationship between the text and the reader, and the rhetorical effects of the experimental novel; if we are to assess the political ideas in these works, then we must describe the propositions that they present – implicitly or explicitly – concerning the nature of authority. Graff tells us that "to determine the politics of any theory, we must look at the way it functions in particular social circumstances" (in Mitchell, *Politics of Interpretation* 133). Well, to determine how an experimental novel promotes its ideology, we must look at the way it functions rhetorically, attempting to engage the attention of a reader and provoking one, through suasive tactics, to an acceptance or rejection of beliefs. I must emphasize that I am not simply interested in rhetorical form *qua* form, but rhetoric as it serves the presentation of power structures in society. In other words, I am interested in the connection between the rhetorical form – i.e., addresser-addressee forms – and the novel's propositions concerning authority.

IMAGINING RHETORICAL INTERACTIONS: WHAT IS AN AUTHOR?

The rhetorical analyses of the novels presented in this book are partly inspired by Wayne Booth's ethical criticism, Roger Fowler's approach to literature through a *social-discourse* model, and George Dillon's deconstructive identification of the codes of social engagement in *Rhetoric as Social Imagination*. Although these theorists end up with different and sometimes contradictory assumptions about the nature of rhetorical "authorship," they do provide important starting-points in forming our critical procedures.

In Booth's classic work of rhetorical literary criticism, *The Rhetoric of Fiction*, clarity of intention is, to use Burke's terms, a "god term." Booth's *Rhetoric* seeks to identify those features of rhetoric in novels that enhance or clarify an author's intentions or purposes. He argues that all fiction is fundamentally rhetorical and argues against the various realist prejudices that frown on explicit authorial intervention in the text: the objective presentation, the unmediated description of life, is impossible, for novels are written by people who have value-laden points of view. An author's "very choice of what he tells will betray him to the reader," and the "author's judgement is always present, always evident to "anyone who knows how to look for it" (*Rhetoric* 20). Though the real author's intentions might be inaccessible, the second "self" that the real author creates to narrate the work of literature is a discernible promoter of values.

Roger Fowler's critical philosophy is similar to Booth's: Fowler acknowledges that he is indebted to the socio-linguistic functionalism of M.A.K. Halliday, whose major assumption is that "the particular form taken by the grammatical system of language is closely related to the social and personal needs that language is required to serve" (in Lyons, *New Horizons* 142). Fowler shares this basic assumption concerning the important connection between form and ideological interest; in *Literature as Social Discourse* he argues that "different varieties or registers within one language enshrine variant world views. Speaking or writing in a variety articulates its own view of the world, and that articulation is a social practice, a conscious or unconscious intervention in the organization of society" (8). Hence, Fowler's social-discourse model does not treat literature as a hermetic artefact but as an articulator of ideology or world-views. The properties of language that reflect the ideology of the writer are the *discourse* elements or the interactional dimensions of texts: "In fiction, the linguistics of discourse applies most naturally to point of view, the author's rhetorical stance towards his narrator, towards his characters (and other elements of content), towards his assumed readers" (*Linguistics and the Novel* 52).

Fowler's illumination of the interactional or interpersonal dimensions of literature provides us with important targets for ideological analysis. He observes that "much communication is concerned with establishing and maintaining unequal power relationships between individuals, between institutions and individuals" (*Literature as Social Discourse* 29). Fowler's views on ideology and the role of criticism are based on three propositions. First, the world of perception and cognition is "an artifice, a social construct" (24). Second, the nature of society is such that it distributes power unequally between classes. Third, the purpose of criticism is to liberate consciousness from the roles and institutions maintained through linguistic control – literature itself is a form of criticism to the extent that it defamiliarizes the language of dominant ideologies and opposes them with counter-ideologies. As critics we can deconstruct the texts that uncritically reproduce the elements of the dominant ideology, or we can interpret counter-ideological texts in a favourable light. Fowler defines ideology here as "a system of beliefs which has come to be constructed as a way of comprehending the world. No person can engage with the world without the cognitive support of ideology in this sense. Ideology cannot be removed. It can be replaced – by alternative ideology. Criticism demonstrates that there are ideologies; compares their structural characteristics, their geneses, their consequence; [it]cannot disperse them" (26).

In *Linguistics and the Novel* Fowler acknowledges Booth's notion that stories cannot be told "without authorial intervention" but disagrees with the distinction between the "real writer who eats his breakfast and then sits down with pen or typewriter" (64) and the implied author or narrative persona that is created in the fiction. Biographical information is relevant for analysis of the implicit speaker that produces the text, and "it would be absurd to discuss Solzhenitsyn's novels without reference to his political views and his personal experiences in Stalin's Russia" (79). Fowler's implicit speaker is a persona situated by the text who adopts a stance towards the reader; the text, which situates the writer, also contains structures that situate the reader.

How does the style of the experimental novel fit with, or perhaps contradict, the implicit message regarding ideology presented by the writer? What does the experimental writer's attitude to the reader tell us about the former's world-view? Is the reader in an experimental text "liberated"? Is one led to a position of compliance, scepticism, or mystification?

In analysing the experimental novel, one must pay attention to how the writer creates a "network of voices at different levels, each presenting a distinct mode of consciousness: the I-figure narrating, the characters, the implied author who controls both narrator and characters, and who often takes a line on them" (*Linguistics* 76). In other words, we must consider the style of the narrator, how characters are presented, and how the beliefs of the implied speaker are manifest.

In this study the discourse relations between author and reader and between the implied author and the various narrators are particularly important. Recognizing that any analysis of authorial ideology is a topic of important contemporary debate concerning subjectivity, I must make it clear at this point that when I refer to the "author" I mean the "implied author," or the textually constructed author. Moreover, the analyses of levels of discourse in this study must obviously begin from my own particular perspective as a critical reader, and, to come full circle back to the idea of a resistant reading suggested by David Bartholomae and Anthony Petrosky's *Ways of Reading*, I must emphasize that reading is an imaginative act.

Much recent discussion of contemporary fiction, specifically criticism of self-reflexive or metafictional novels, emphasizes the freedom of the reader in the production of literary meaning. Linda Hutcheon describes the liberating effect of contemporary metafiction in *Narcissistic Narrative*: "To read is to act; to act is both to interpret and to create anew – to be revolutionary, perhaps in political as well as literary terms. There is much freedom-inducing potential in metafiction generally" (161). Hutcheon defends contemporary experiments with self-reflexivity because such works are ideologically self-aware and this awareness is transferred to the reading reader. According to Hutcheon, the contemporary reader no longer regards the author as a privileged and idealized consciousness that speaks with utter authority in the romantic sense; but at the same time, the inherently *subjective* nature of fictional discourse is insistently shown by self-conscious novels. The author has been shown to be a textually encoded position in a discursive situation that always includes an enunciating addresser as well as a receiver of the utterance: "The Romantic 'author,' as originating and original source of meaning, may well be dead, as Roland Barthes argued years ago, but his position – one of discursive authority – remains, and increasingly is the focus of much contemporary literature and also much theoretical debate" (xv).

Hutcheon proceeds to argue that the emphasis on the "interactive powers involved in the production and reception of texts" in metafiction revolutionizes the roles of reader and writer because the reader is turned "into a collaborator instead of a consumer" and "the artist reappears, not as God-like Romantic creator, but as the inscribed maker of a social product that has the potential to participate in social change through its reader" (*Narcissistic Narrative* xv–xvi). The self-conscious narrator in metafiction, says Hutcheon, can demystify power by revealing its "arbitrariness, to allow Calvino's narrator at the start of *If on a Winter's Night a Traveller* to order the reader around, for instance ... In other words, a text can call attention to authority structures in such a way as to subvert the Romantic ideology of the myth of originality that once subtended them" (xvi).

I agree with Hutcheon that metafiction can demystify power and that there is a "freedom-inducing potential" that results from being a "collaborator" in the making of a metafictional narrative; however, sometimes this freedom comes from being able to resist the role that we are being scripted to play, as in the kinds of ironic rhetorical readings that a reader trained in George Dillon's codes is able to enact. As Hutcheon says, "the 'author' becomes a position to be filled, a role to be inferred, by the reader reading the text. When we speak of producers and receivers of literary language, then, we speak less of individual subjects than of what have been called 'subject positions' that are essential constitutive features of the work" (*Narcissistic Narrative* xvi). But while Hutcheon emphasizes that the reader of metafiction is "liberated" and the author is no longer the "manipulating 'author' as a person," she still recognizes that readers are constrained by the structures created by the author, for "the reader never really creates literary meaning freely; there are codes and rules and conventions that underlie its production. Selection and isolation procedures are inevitably restricting, but they are also necessary" (*Narcissistic Narrative* 152).

Hutcheon emphasizes that the reader is free to complete the "open work" of fiction. My own interest is in how the "codes and rules and conventions" built into the work to ensure its "inner coherence" compel the reader to place herself or himself in a particular state of reception, as a "pre-positioned reader," and to perceive the author in a particular position relative to the narrative and to the reader as a "pre-positioned author."

I have adopted the concepts of the pre-positioned author and reader from Bernard Sharratt's *Reading Relations*. Sharratt describes the systems of relations between authors and readers as being made up of a number of positions in the writing and reading process. The following list of author and reader positions has been adapted from his model:

Four senses of "author"
1 Author: a position within the relation Author-Publisher;
2 *author*: the one who *writes* the text ...;
3 AUTHOR: occupying a Textual Position as posited by the *author*;
4 Textual Author: occupying a Textual Position constructed by a *reader*.

Three senses of "reader"
1 *reader*: the one who *reads* the text ...;
2 READER: the occupier of a Textual Position constructed by the act of *reading*;
3 Textual Reader: the reader-position posited by the *author* in the act of *writing*.   (87)

In my analysis of literature as social discourse, the AUTHOR, Textual Author, READER, and Textual Reader positions receive the most attention. In theory these relations can be separated and the positions seen as distinct; but a pragmatic rhetorical description of the author's writing might combine analysis of the *author*'s positing of his or her position and the Textual Reader in the text with analysis of the *reader*'s reading of and reaction to the *author*'s rhetoric and ideology. *A critical reading illuminates a double positioning: that of the writer and that of the reader.*

Booth's notion of the implied author and Fowler's implicit speaker have been radically problematized by anti-intentionalist critiques referred to by Hutcheon, including Roland Barthes's "Death of the Author" and Michel Foucault's seminal essay "What Is an Author?" Donald Pease notes that the demotion of the author, in the wake of the New Criticism's attempts to isolate the formal features of texts – symptomatized by the ideas of the intentional and affective fallacies – has resulted in a new interpretive game for readers. Pease writes, "In order to separate the text from contamination by an author, such newer critics as Roland Barthes have declared the author dead. By the 'author,' Barthes means the demands – for psychological consistency, meaning, unity – that an autonomous subject would exact from a textual environment. In the wake of the author's death, Barthes has proposed a new definition of literature: a discursive game always arriving at the limits of its own rule, without any author other than the reader (or 'scriptor' as Barthes refers to him), who is defined as an effect of the writing game he activates" (in Lentricchia, *Critical Terms* 112). The role of the critic then becomes of primary importance in the construction of meaning; it is this emphasis on the reader's control of rhetorical meaning that is the focus of Georges Dillon's *Rhetoric as Social Imagination*.

DILLON'S FOOTINGS

In Dillon's work the composing activity is a mode of imagined inter-action. Writers imagine a social relationship between themselves and an addressee, and script their authorial role as well as that of the reader "out of bits of social and linguistic codes" (*Rhetoric as Social Imagination* 15). The social relationship that writers script between themselves and their imagined audience is what Dillon calls a "footing" (17). He describes five kinds of these footings which are more precise concepts for denoting what has traditionally been called *tone*: 1) impersonal/personal: a scale marked by either the absence or presence of a scripted involvement between the writer's self (marked by the *I* pronoun) and the reader (marked by *you*); 2) distant/solidary: the degree to which the writer either evades or moves towards a common ground or shared values with the reader (often through the use of *we*); 3) superior/equal: a scale that measures whether the writer assumes a greater wisdom or equal knowledge in relation to the imagined reader; 4) confrontive/oblique: the degree to which the writer is able to be blunt, forthright, or confrontive with the reader, or needs to be carefully indirect to spare the feelings of the addressee; 5) formal/informal: the scale of stylistic conventions that distinguish calculated and patterned prose from spontaneous and casual utterance. An author may continually fluctuate in the use of these footings, using one approach that is "impersonal" at one moment, then "personal" the next. Writers create several footings and imagine several relationships with readers, from the informal and friendly to the distant and impersonal. Dillon analyses the footings or codes of engagement used in various kinds of popular advice books, including books on child-rearing, sex education, writing, and dieting.

In Dillon's analysis, relationships are conceived of in competitive terms, "the relation of Writer and Reader as analyzable into somewhat metaphorical vectors of approval and distance or aggression and ingratiation" (17). While acknowledging the influence on his theory of the agonistic view of rhetoric presented by Walter Ong, Richard Lanham, and Kenneth Burke, Dillon is interested in how

Machiavellian motives may underlie the tone of co-operation and open-mindedness that professional advice-givers adopt. In examining books by authors such as Dale Carnegie, Manuel Smith, and William Coles, Dillon assesses whether these books deal with readers in a way that is consistent with the advice they give concerning the management of human relationships. Carnegie and Smith are described as promoters of a *soft* rhetoric in their advice books, "a mode that avoids overt verbal agressiveness, such as sarcasm and criticism, even 'arguing' itself, and that advocates indirection and self-effacement" (44). Yet soft rhetoric is still devious: "More flies are caught with honey than with gall, Carnegie reminds us, but after all it is business as usual: one is still catching flies" (57).

The fear of imposition or enslavement and the desire to gain approval, esteem, and admiration in social interactions are the conflicting impulses that are brought into harmony through Dillon's view of rhetoric. The rhetor's challenge is to order the auditors, command them, or impose a belief on them (to violate the negative face wants, or the need to be free from impositions) while feeding their need for approval and admiration (catering to positive face wants). The rhetor attempts to change the auditors while assuring them that they are really worthy listeners. In another exposure of rhetorical sleight-of-hand Dillon describes how Richard Bolles's vocational self-help book *What Colour Is Your Parachute?* tries to convince the reader that action will change the reader's life; but Bolles traps the reader in passive list-making and chart-drawing exercises that increase passivity rather than initiate real action.

Dillon's procedures for the rhetorical unpacking of authorial footings draw their assumptions from the contemporary critique of representation found in Derrida and Foucault. In Dillon's fourth chapter on "Who Writes? The Codes of Authority," he cites Roland Barthes's *The Pleasure of the Text*: "As institution, the author is dead," though, ironically, we " *desire* the author, need his figure" (91). Dillon shares with post-structuralist critiques of speech-act linguistics a scepticism concerning authorial presence. Putting the author as subject in question, sharing with Foucault's essay "What Is an Author?" the notion that the concept of the author is an abstract contextual principle that limits the meaning of an utterance, Dillon's rhetorical analyses undermine the metaphysics of authorial presence.

At first this shattering of the illusion of presence would seem to undermine some of the major principles of rhetoric: does not the traditional triangular communication model have an addresser-addressee dynamic at its core? But Dillon rereads classical rhetoric so that it can in fact accommodate the post-structuralist critique of representation and presence. Dillon argues that unlike the Platonic rhetor, the Aristotelian rhetor does not believe that an essential self is projected in speech or writing. The "self" presented to an audience is a *constructed* self, one that is tailored to the persuasive demands of the occasion, the audience's beliefs, and the speaker's purpose. The self that is constructed is then *inferred* by the audience, whose procedures of inference may or may not approximate what the rhetor envisaged as their preferred procedures.

Rhetoric thus is always susceptible to misreading and appropriation. An ideal rhetoric would try to minimize its misuse by the audience and keep the construction-inference process in line with the rhetor's intention through effective rhetorical scriptings – the footings – that ingratiate the audience and compel them to play the social-relationship game that the rhetor wants them to play.

Dillon's rhetorical analyses undermine the metaphysics of authorial presence held by traditional rhetoric. But this is *not* anti-rhetorical; it is a move that simply recovers a belief that is implicit in Aristotle and the technical rhetorics developed by the Sophists who preceded him. Dillon, like Lanham, Derrida, and Foucault, acknowledges what Aristotle knew all along: *ethos* and *pathos* are not essential dimensions of the "self" but are the "imagined" products of audience interpretations, and these interpretations may be constrained by linguistic and rhetorical conventions; however, such conventions do not guarantee the uniform inference of ethos and pathos.

In a dazzling deconstructive move that begins by concurring with the Barthesian idea that the author is "dead," or that the parental conceiver of writing is absent (an absence acknowledged by Socrates in his criticism of the unsituated free-play of interpretation to which written texts can be subjected because of the absence of the real author as interlocutor and defender of his own utterance), Dillon is able to move to the final outcome: the "death" of the reader (149).

Readers might have roles scripted for them in a text, but that is no guarantee that they will play the role. As Dillon notes, his own responses to the advice books that he rhetorically criticizes do not control his responses but postulate a "ghost" reader: rhetoric is the imaginary construction of a footing cultivated by an imaginary author for the imaginary role the reader is expected to play. Only reading itself breathes life into the "dead author" and "dead reader": reading constructs their social relations.

Early in his book Dillon disclaims or limits any special privilege for his rhetorical criticism of texts. What he offers is not "a scientific or objective or causative account of why we respond as we do to various texts" but rather "a sketch of the frameworks that writers offer us within which actual responses occur" (20): as he writes, "our responses to the passages cited below are colored by an analytic interest; we do not read them with the purpose for which they were intended ... our response is then to some degree an imaginary one or one based on an imaginary premise – as perhaps more of our responses are than we think" (20). It is *this special way of reading*, an imaginative way of constructing the footings and the addressee-addresser relations of fictional texts, that informs the rhetorical interventions in the rest of this book.

For this investigation I have chosen six innovative Canadian novels that have received significant critical attention. *The Double Hook* (1959) is a conspicuously non-naturalist or post-realist novel that mythologizes the psychology of power struggles in family relations. *Beautiful Losers* (1966) contains many of the traits of North American avantgarde writing of the sixties: surrealism, psychedelic excess, bizarre comedy, a collage of images from popular culture, as well as a spirit of political and sexual rebellion. *The New Ancestors* (1970) is an important work because it is one of the earliest English Canadian novels that explores colonialism and the growth of political independence in African culture; as well, Godfrey is an obvious literary experimenter who makes bold use of difficult and tangled narrative structures that frustrate easy paraphrase and plot summary. *Badlands* (1975), written by an important supporter of Canadian postmodern critical theory, addresses some of the most controversial issues facing the writer of the seventies and eighties: the problematic relationships between fiction and reality and between storytellers and audiences, and the politics of sex. *Burning Water* (1980) is a species of post-realist metafiction, that genre of contemporary fiction that is self-reflexive and often engages directly in a dialogue with other discourses; like *Badlands* it is a novel that explores the nature of fiction and the authority structures of the past. *The Handmaid's Tale* (1985) is a didactic novel, a satiric dystopia in the tradition of Zamyatin's *We* or Orwell's *Nineteen Eighty-four*. I have included this novel because it is so conspicuous in its interest in sexual politics and authority and because I think that Atwood, one of the best-known contemporary Canadian writers, although she is not normally classified as an "experimenter," has managed in this work to rewrite quite brilliantly the Zamyatin and Orwell allegories from a specifically female perspective. This rewriting is a particularly post-realist and innovative gesture, and it merits critical engagement.

The six novels are thus a sample of the forms of post-realist English Canadian fiction from 1959 to 1985; they have been selected because they are conspicuously innovative and strong in the forms, techniques, and concepts that can compel, sustain, and withstand the critical interventions of this particular rhetorical critic and his foray with them into the Canadian critical parlour.

2 *The Double Hook*: Miracle, Mystery, and Authority

The Double Hook mythologizes the psychology of the power conflicts that exist in that most basic of social organizations: the family. Conflicts between child and parent, between husband and wife, between families and their kin or neighbours are presented in terms of the emotional consequences that such conflicts have: the paranoia of the family elders, the rancour in the young whose desires are obstructed, and the jealousy of family members who have been excluded from love, who lack the fertility of others, or who suspect the infidelity of their mates or kin. The unfolding drama of these familial conflicts is powerfully magnified into grand mythic proportions through the use of an incantatory rhetorical voice, which syntactically and lexically echoes the Old Testament; the drama of family conflict is also rendered mysterious, ambiguous, and often obscure by the blending of the different symbols and archetypal patterns from Old Testament and American Indian myth.

As evidence of the resonant layering of these elements, the critical conversation in the Canadian Burkean parlour that has attended and constructed *The Double Hook* concentrates on the identification and interpretation of symbols and archetypes; even those critics who have focused on Watson's language have produced exegeses that are designed to make the text more intelligible, ignoring the discourse elements in the novel that militate against rational analysis. (See Northey, Lennox, Mitchell, and Monkman in George Bowering's collection of the major criticism, *Sheila Watson and The Double Hook.*)

Indeed, most of the critical effort has not dealt with the imagined *effect* of "Watson's" language on the reader. (It should be noted that the use of an author's name here and elsewhere in this study refers to the literary and critically constructed author. In Foucault's sense, the author's name is a useful and inescapable rubric that we have used to stabilize, unify, classify, and limit the texts that are inaugurated, by their titles and authors, in our critical conversations.) After I, as a rhetorically minded reader, identify the biblical tone, the name of an Indian trickster god, the Arthurian implications of fishing and the "Waste Land" imagery, and the spiritual significance of specific acts (Greta's suicide, or Kip's blinding, for example), my own interpretive stance as a critic, reader, and rhetor compels me to ask *how* and *why* I can imagine particular authoritative and oblique footings. How is my imagining of the rhetorical interaction scripted by the compelling language of Sheila Watson?

The Double Hook immerses the reader in a world whose ontological status is mysterious and resistant to rational understanding. The imagined author's metaphysical and aesthetic assumptions, or her ideology, can be inferred from the prophetic mode of discourse that the narrator uses and from the way in which this implied author presents actions and settings. In the world of *The Double Hook*, a world where spiritual deities watch over the affairs of men and in which geography is simultaneously literal and figurative, the actions of characters are often motivated by ineffable emotion or are mysteriously compelled by divine influence. This is a world in which I can imagine people as capable of having spiritual visions and in which the conflicts and power struggles between members of society spring from the obscure depths of desire and feeling.

Henry Kreisel has remarked that *The Double Hook*, notwithstanding the amount of illuminating critical attention it has received, "retains its mystery, its central core inviolable" (in Bowering, *Sheila Watson* 8). What follows here is a self-conscious attempt to resist and interrogate that mystery, to intervene in the critical conversation and show how the mystery is effected, through what techniques, and for what possible purposes.

THE RHETORICAL FOOTINGS OF THE IMAGINED AUTHOR: THE NARRATOR AS PROPHET, THE WORLD AS MIRACLE

When we begin to read *The Double Hook*, we might first wonder "Where are we?" "What is the nature of this world?" and "Who is

speaking?" In my rhetorical reading, I begin to imagine a social interaction with an implied author:

1   In the folds of the hills
              under Coyote's eye
                    lived

              the old lady, mother of William
                of James and of Greta

              lived James and Greta
              lived William and Ara his wife
              lived the Widow Wagner
              the Widow's girl Lenchen
              the Widow's boy
              lived Felix Prosper and Angel
              lived Theophil
              and Kip

                    until one morning in July

Greta was at the stove. Turning hotcakes. Reaching for the coffee beans.
Grinding away James's voice.
    James was at the top of the stairs. His hand half-raised. His voice in the
rafters.
    James walking away. The old lady falling. There under the jaw of the roof.
In the vault of the bed loft. Into the shadow of death. Pushed by James's will.
By James's hand. By James's words: This is my day. You'll not fish today.

2 Still the old lady fished. If the reeds had dried up and the banks folded and
crumbled down she would have fished still.

                                        The Double Hook 19–20

    When I take careful account of how I imagine the implied author
of the novel, I am struck by how I am initially positioned in a world
where human action has no apparent effect, for action and the objects
of action have been strangely divorced, and agents or initiators of
actions have also been separated. The opening authorial voice – in a
tone that George Dillon would classify as impersonal, distant, authoritative, and oblique – expresses itself in incantatory and biblical

rhythms that are produced by the anaphora and parallelism in these lines, especially in the serial listing of the characters (see Godard, in Bowering, on the tense sequences associated with character). But what is most obviously striking, after the graphological arrangement of the lines to resemble free verse, is the fragmenting of the normal sentence. Many of the sentence fragments in the first section are participial phrases that are detached from their antecedent subject; however, because of the parallel arrangement of the phrases, the elliptical connection to "Greta" is functionally obvious in the fragments "Turning hotcakes. Reaching for the coffee beans. Grinding away James's voice." The *effect* of these fragments is the unnatural isolation of the verbal element, the act, as it hovers unattached to an agent. The auxiliary verb "was" indicates the past tense of the action, though the *aspect* of the verb, the durational quality of the activity, is *ongoing* because of the "ing" ending. In effect, the separation of the main verb from the auxiliary that indicates tense results in a confusion of which acts have been completed and which are ongoing, and what temporal point of reference the acts are relative to.

The suppression of the auxiliary verb "was," along with the absence of subordination, functions to obscure the narration of James's killing of his mother. The effect of the following passage changes markedly when we insert some auxiliary verbs, and subordinators, and make explicit the object of James's actions – though there is still a disjunction between action and object that can only be eliminated by a complete rearrangement of Watson's sentences:

[When] James was at the top of the stairs[,] His hand [was] half-raised. His voice [was] in the rafters.
James [was] walking away [as] The old lady [was] falling. There under the jaw of the roof. In the vault of the bed loft. Into the shadow of death. [The old lady was] Pushed by James's will. By James's hand.

Watson's presentation creates a sense of disconnection between cause and effect, agent and act, act and consequence. The factual violence of James's act is mitigated, embellished and rendered as a ritualistic violence that is spiritually significant: he pushes his mother into the "jaw," "bed loft," or "the shadow of death." And yet this act is reduced in physical potency, cut short, and rendered inconsequential. In comic defiance the old lady appears in the next section: "Still the old lady fished." Hence, James's attempt to rebel is presented as ineffectual, an action that cannot be successfully fulfilled.

In the opening pages of *The Double Hook* Watson emphasizes the inefficacy of human action. Even innocent domestic acts are presented in a manner that stresses the passive nature of the human agent:

Ara went to the door. She threw the water from the basin into the dust. She watched the water roll in balls on the ground.
    Roll and divide and spin.   (22)

In order to show how Watson's language reinforces a sense of the passivity and exhaustion of the community and its spiritual aridity, a condition that compels a quest for redemption, some readers of *The Double Hook* have emphasized Watson's use of "Waste Land" imagery. Aside from figurative language, however, one of the most powerful techniques that Watson employs to emphasize the inertia and spiritual torpor of the community is the juxtaposition of points of view, especially the views of gods and men, and the conflation of discourse levels. Human acts of perception appear diminutive and inconsequential when compared to the awesome powers of the divine entities that hover over and control the land:

Ara looked over the fence. There was no one on the road. It lay across the burnt grass.
    Coyote made the land his pastime. He stretched out his paw. He breathed on the grass. His spittle eyed it with prickly pear.   (22)

Coyote's significance as a trickster figure in American Indian mythology and as a satanic deity whose cruelty must be mitigated by a quest for redemption has been discussed by Leslie Monkman. However, in Monkman's analysis, certain metaphysical assumptions made by the text are simply accepted without an interrogation of their rhetorical effect on the reader. While we must grant that Coyote represents a catalogue of meanings, though not necessarily in the satanic sense of Monkman's study, which privileges a Christian interpretation and world-view over an Indian one, I prefer to emphasize *how* Watson uses Coyote to reinforce the metaphysics of the world of the text.

The primary *function* of Coyote is not as an allegorical figure but as a reified deity who wields power over the land and watches over, influences, and comments on the lives of the characters. The presence of such a deity, whose status is not simply abstract, reflects the metaphysical assumptions of the implied author in *The Double Hook*: this is a metaphysics that is part of a modernist inheritance from romanticism, a longing for spiritual immanence, a desire for pantheistic plenitude (see Eagleton, *Criticism and Ideology* 148; Booth, *Critical*

Understanding 143–9). That Coyote is not just a symbolic figure, but is more importantly a reified entity who hovers over the world is reinforced by depictions of the planet of men as a small particle that is bathed in a mysterious spiritual light: "Outside the world floated like a mote in a straight shaft of glory"(26).

While the surveillance of a deity like Coyote reinforces our sense that the landscape of *The Double Hook* is charged with an inscrutable and capricious spiritual presence, the perceptions of natural forces also reinforce this sense: characters are often shown as seeing natural forces animated by a presence that is violent and savage. When Ara, caught outside by the storm, is forced to take shelter in the home of Greta Potter, Watson presents the storm in the lexis of the cattle-drive. The storm rendered in such figurative terms is not, however, simply a form of pathetic fallacy, a symbol of the violence about to be unleashed upon the community by James and Greta, but is presented as Ara's apprehension of a fantastic phenomenal world:

Overhead the sky was tight as rawhide. About them the bars of the earth darkened. The flat ribs of the hills ...

Kip's face was turned to the sky. To the light stampeded together and bawling before the massed darkness. The white bulls of the sky shoulder to shoulder ...

Ara looked up too. For a minute she saw the light. Then only the raw skin of the sky drawn over them like a sack.

Then the rain swung into the mouth of the valley like a web. Strand to strand. The sky, Ara thought, filled with adder tongues. With lariats. With bull-whips.

She reached the porch before the first lash hit the far side of the house.   (35–6)

The presentation of the storm scene shows the conflation of the implied author's discourse and the perceptions of a character. This collapsing of points of view, a technique that Watson uses frequently, correlates the author's supernaturally charged reality with the perceptions of Ara. Thus, again validated as fantastic phenomenon and not as metaphor, the setting of *The Double Hook* is rendered surreal or supernatural. The implied author's pronouncements on the animacy of the natural world are fused with the subjective impressions of characters, lending the latter the same irrefutable authority as the former. It is the implied author, of course, who constructs the explicit comparisons, "the sky ... tight as rawhide" or "the sky drawn over them like a sack" or "the rain swung ... like a web"; it is, however, less clear whether the implied author is depicting the storm or is rendering the subjective thoughts of Kip when the storm clouds, "light stampeded together and bawling," are implicitly compared to a herd of "white bulls ... shoulder to shoulder." In this case there is a conflation of the discourse levels of author and character; more importantly, the implied author's authoritative footing is used to emphasize the animate nature of the storm, not just its symbolic tenor, the violent power of storms in general. The "beast" vehicle has become more important than its signified tenor.

Ara's figurative perception of the storm is similarly cast into literal terms by the commentary of the narrator. The narrator's point of view is conflated with Ara's as the narrator shows how she "looked up" and "saw the light"; her perceptions are rendered in the third-person voice of the narrator. Yet this voice subtly gives way to Ara's fragmented and imagistic first-person thought. Moving from the menace of the "adder tongues," then shifting to the more threatening sense of capture or imprisonment connoted by "lariats," her "thought," her metaphoric translation of the storm, finally climaxes with the sense of the physical punishment of the lashing "bull-whips." When the implied author describes Ara arriving at the Potter's door, however, the narrator does not stray from the literal phenomenon as felt by her: "She reached the porch before the first *lash* hit the far side of the house."

What I am attempting to illustrate are the effects – on my own rhetorical interpretive activity – of Watson's persistent literalization of the metaphors that depict natural forces: Watson literalizes the metaphor to emphasize how the world of *The Double Hook* is ruled by ineffable spiritual powers. The presentation of Lenchen's perception of the storm demonstrates the same narrative tactic. The physical storm, which is a figurative anticipation of James's whipping of Lenchen and Greta, is perceived in an extravagantly sensuous way by Lenchen. This passage exemplifies yet again the literalization of metaphor:

In the sky above evil had gathered strength. It took body writhing and twisting under the high arch. Lenchen could hear the breath of it in the pause. The swift indrawing. The silence of the contracting muscle. The head drop for the wild plunge and hoof beat of it.
    She leant forward a little.
    I wanted Angel, she said. But she's not at Theophil's.   (41)

Here the physical storm, which is simultaneously an abstract embodiment of "evil," is perceived as an animal being, for Lenchen "hears" its exertions as it strains to lunge through the air.

There is a complex compounding of metaphors, a catachresis, in this passage. The abstract tenor is "evil," but the vehicle for this abstract concept is both a literal storm and something animal. Normally, such an ingenious conceit of this type clarifies the nature of the tenor by showing the points of resemblance between it – in this case, evil – and the vehicles. Here the storm, now nominally evil, gathers "strength" and manifests itself as a sensuously "twisting" movement in an obscure, non-visualized space ("It took body writhing and twisting under the high arch"), and as we read, we momentarily register the two possible forms of the verb "took" as transitive and intransitive, indicating the meaning of both "taking shape" and "wrestling with the body of another." Notions of metamorphosis and struggle are thus merged. In the third sentence, however, we are given an image of movement only as an implication of its product, the sound of a "breath." Again, the location and shape of the implied vehicle of comparison, some animal form, is suppressed, kept mysterious and ominous. We do not apprehend where this entity is in space, nor what it looks like, but we can feel and hear the passionate – almost sexual – movement of its plunging muscles because of the sounds, movements, and bodily qualities suggested by the language ("breath," "swift indrawing," "contracting muscle," "head drop," "wild plunge," "hoof beat") and the climactic build-up in the increasing length of the sentences: "The swift indrawing. The silence of the contracting muscle. The head drop for the wild plunge and hoof beat of it."

The suggestion of sensual, urgent, animal movement is thus kept in the dimensions of hearing and bodily sense; the lack of visual imagery shrouds the subject in a darkness, increases the sense of tension and sexual suggestiveness, and above all shifts the moral concept of "evil" on to a plane of mysteriousness. The passage is constructed to reinforce the sense that the things of our world cannot be understood cognitively, that they are unpredictable and unlocatable: evil can come charging out of the darkness at any time, like the storm, like Lenchen's desire, or James's revolt.

In presenting Lenchen's perception of the storm, Watson again uses the technique of conflating the points of view of the implied author and the character. The implied author begins by asserting the metaphorical connection between the landscape and an abstract concept – the storm and evil – and then shifts to the inner consciousness of Lenchen without distinguishing between the narrator's assertion and the impressions of the character. This is but further evidence that the implied author's construction of the landscape as mysterious is always borne out by the beliefs and apprehensions of characters. The ontological status of events is never demystified by the voice of the implied author; in fact, it is the metaphysical nominalist like Theophil, arguing that "There's no big Coyote, like you think" (57), who is made to appear blind to reality, not the characters who have spiritual "visions."

THE IRRATIONALIZATION OF HUMAN ACTION

The irrational nature of existence in *The Double Hook* is also emphasized by the prominence of instinct and transcendence in the actions of characters. James is a good example. Treated by some critics as an archeypal hero on a "quest," James actually stumbles from one act to another, purposeless and blind, unaware of why he does anything at all, getting by on pure instinct, luck, and some external guidance; he is markedly unlike the hero of the traditional quest myth and more akin to the picaresque rogue.

After presenting James as the rebel "murderer" and the scourge of Kip, Greta, and Ara, Watson shows him struggling with the meaning of his actions and wanting to escape responsibility. Having fled his home territory and arrived in town, James sees "a single sinuous curve of the river, the shadows of the clouds passing over the water as the shadow of the branches had lain for a moment on Lenchen's throat." He wants to throw himself into the "long arms" of the river, but again sees the ghostly presence of his mother, "the brown figure he sought to escape": "He asked himself now for the first time what he'd really intended to do when he'd defied his mother at the head of the stairs" (98).

James' acts of violence against his mother, Kip, Greta, and Lenchen are obliquely presented, obscurely motivated, and seemingly purposeless. His actions in the town are equally unguided: he withdraws his money, buys travelling gear from the general store, then falls into the company of the con-man Traff. Throughout his "quest" in the world of men, James appears as the object of the machinations of others, still observed and frightened by his mother's spirit, manipulated by Traff, and robbed by Felicia. It is, in fact, the actions of these strangers that force him to abandon his escape and return to Lenchen and his home community:

James looked back over his shoulder at the moonlight slanting on the roof of Felicia's shack. There where the moonlight slid down the walls Traff and Lilly swam in the pool of silver they had stolen.

The flick of a girl's hand had freed James from freedom. He'd kissed away escape in the mud by the river. He thought now of Lenchen and the child who would wear his face. Alone on the edge of town where men clung together for protection, he saw clearly for a moment his simple hope.   (121)

Even James's return is depicted as fortuitous or guided by the mysterious instincts of the horse upon which he rides, as the rider himself shuts his eyes and simply clings to the back of his animal. James is not responsible for his own return – his remarkable horse is:

At the bottom they came to a creek. James could hear the horse's feet parting the water. He could hear the flow of water on stones, but in this skyless slit the water was opaque and formless. He shut his eyes and fastened his free hand in his horse's mane.

As they climbed again, the horse seemed to draw life with every breath. It climbed. It rounded ledges. It held close to the rock where nothing but the feel of stone marked the fall below.   (122)

When James finally returns and sees the destroyed family home, he senses an opportunity to build anew; however, Watson again emphasizes the mysterious fortuitousness of his return, for "by some generous gesture he had been turned once more into the first pasture of things" (131). When William asks James why Greta destroyed the home, James initially seems able to clarify the origins of the conflict, the motives for the rebellion, for "God knows, he said, we both had reason to wish the place gone and everything in it" (132). But there ends the articulation of his "reasons." His actions are presented as an irrationally followed circle of light and darkness, love and hate, escape and return. What has James accomplished?:

James turned to the boy. What could he say of the light that had made him want to drink fire into his darkness. Of the child got between the leafless trees when the frost was stiff in the branches. Of beating up Kip and running off because Kip had been playing around with the glory of the world.

I ran away, he said, but I circled and ended here the way a man does when he's lost.   (132)

James's sense of the lack of control over his own actions finds company in the irrational impulses of all of the other characters and in the way they construe the origins of their actions. To apologize to Lenchen for making a pass at her, Kip blames the effects of planetary influence: "Tell the girl ... that I didn't mean nothing. The old white moon had me by the hair" (116). And Ara says, to Widow Wagner, who believes that suffering is the inevitable consequence of sin, that moral conduct has no bearing on our condition in this world: "Right and wrong don't make much difference ... We don't choose what we will suffer. We can't even see how suffering will come" (119). Yet again, the agents in this world are shown as helpless to control their own destinies.

The "seeing" or insight that is experienced by many of the characters is not of a historical-social kind, not cognitive, not abstract, but intuitive and prophetic. Again, it is part of the mystification strategy of the novel to present seemingly symbolic experiences in a manner that emphasizes the literal spiritual transformation that takes place. Turned into supernatural event and miracle, the abstract symbolic level is literalized in the form of the ghost of an old lady that haunts the landscape and the voice of an unpredictable god that calls down to the people. Even such nominally symbolic characters as Felix Prosper have transcendental experiences that are significant more because of their miraculous nature than their symbolic referentiality:

It was not until the girl had come battering at his peace that he'd wondered at all about the pain of a growing root ... If he could only shed his flesh, moult and feather again, he might begin once more.

His eyelids dropped. His flesh melted. He rose from the bed on soft owl wings. And below he saw his old body crouched down like an ox by the manger. (126)

The conventional exegeses of *The Double Hook* would excavate the Christian allusions in such a scene and would remind us of the Christian paradox of fall and redemption echoed in "Felix" (*felix culpa*). But having identified Felix with some priestly function, and having cast the birth of Lenchen's child into the context of the blessed nativity of a "saviour," how can the conventional criticism of myth and archetype account for the tensions and contradictions that detract from the "holiness" of the birth and simply obscure its meaning? Lenchen is not a Mary, James not a Joseph, and there are no textual allusions that ineluctably mark them as the parents of a saviour.

The assumption that a birth will automatically unite the community, that such an event automatically mitigates all previous crimes, is not an assumption that will be unanimously granted. Such emblems elicit a reflex response that blinds one to the overall effects of a discourse. What Watson does here is to insert a scene of metamorphosis that is neither just Felix's fantasy, nor just symbolic action, nor just supernatural out-of-body experience: all these are implied, compelling the reader to make the first interpretive move. But the mode that Watson uses is purposely ambiguous. Are the "dropped" eyelids an indicator of daydreaming, a means of bracketing the experience off from reality? Does Felix's body "melt" and transform into some angelic entity? The denotative use of the language compels the reader to treat this passage not as symbol but as miracle. Does Felix perceive his own role as that of an animal attending the birth of a saviour, and is he aware of the explicit comparison with the ox and all its ramifications? Many of Felix's gnomic utterances are shown to be inappropriate formulaic responses – responses he flings out for lack of anything better to say. Whatever Watson means, her text allows for a number of interpretations, all of which enforce a sense of Felix's seeing the world from a new, *heightened* perspective (literally and symbolically) and of his spiritually charged perception of the mysterious moment of nativity upon which he is attending.

Felix Prosper's spiritual experiences are complemented by other moments of transcendence, prophecy, or irrational vision in the lives of characters. Kip, for one, is assigned his share of gnomic utterances on the ambiguities of existence ("you can't catch the glory on a hook and hold on to it. That when you fish for the glory you catch the darkness too. That if you hook twice the glory you hook twice the fear" 61); and Ara is also provided with a number of prophetic insights:

She remembered how she'd thought of water as a death which might seep through the dry shell of the world. Now her tired eyes saw water issuing from under the burned threshold ...

Everything shall live where the river comes, she said out loud. And she saw a great multitude of fish, each fish springing arched through the slanting light.   (114)

It is Ara, we should note, who hears the final words of the coyote deity overseeing the community, a deity who claims responsibility for the fate of Lenchen's child:

Above her the sky stretched like a tent pegged to the broken rock. And from a cleft of the rock she heard the voice of coyote crying down through the boulders:

I have set his feet on soft ground;
I have set his feet on the sloping shoulders
of the world. (134)

The prophetic or visionary experiences of Watson's characters always produce gnomic utterance and ambiguous emblem rather

than propositional meaning; not social forecasts but oblique and im-
pressionistic evidence of the presence and power of the watching deities. These people hear the mysterious, unanswerable utterance of a
coyote and a god. The power of these utterances brings to mind the
statement of the barkeeper in the town, Paddy, who says of his parrot,
"He gets his way because he's unique. Men don't often have their
own way. It's not many have the rights of a dumb beast and a speaking man at the same time" (103). In the world of *The Double Hook* only
gods and speaking parrots can have their own way, because only
they can assert their discourse free from the interference of sceptical
interlocutors.

THE IRRATIONALIZATION OF POWER

Many critics have felt compelled to read *The Double Hook* as a version
of Christian allegory concerning the need for charity, family stability,
and community. Such criticism often fails to uncover how Christian
and Judaic ideology irrationalizes human conflict by presenting
human power struggles as sometimes irreconcilable, as not subject to
resolution through reason. In *The Double Hook* the conflicts seem biblical because they are familial, emotional, and irrational, most often
stemming from the struggle over the control of desire, and competition for love. Erich Auerbach has commented on the nature of conflict
as it is presented through Old Testament ideology, and he contrasts
this to the Greek-Homeric understanding of conflict:

In the Old Testament stories the peace of daily life in the house, in the fields,
and among the flocks, is undermined by jealousy over election and the promise of a blessing, and complications arise which would be utterly incompre-
hensible to the Homeric heroes. The latter must have palpable and clearly
expressible reasons for their conflicts and enmities, and these work themselves out in free battles; whereas, with the former, the perpetually smouldering jealousy and the connection between the domestic and the spiritual,
between the paternal blessing and the divine blessing, lead to daily life being
permeated with the stuff of conflict, often with poison. The sublime influence
of God here reaches so deeply into the everyday that the two realms of the
sublime and the everyday are not only actually unseparated but basically
inseparable.   (*Mimesis* 19)

Power conflicts in *The Double Hook* do arise from "jealousy over
election." One has the sense that this jealousy is indeed perpetually
smouldering, that such enmity is not open to resolution, and that this
dark layer of ineffable rancour reinforces the connection between the

domestic and the spiritual by infusing the irrational elements of the latter into the commonplace world of the former. In the *Double Hook* power struggles occur between parent figures and their children, James and Mrs Potter, Lenchen and Widow Wagner, between brother and sister, James and Greta, and between lovers. In each case the struggle is over who can control love and desire.

In the Potter family, enmity grows out of the silences, the unarticulated and unresolved competitions between family members. The Potters live "suspended in silence," and "when they spoke they spoke of hammers and buckles, of water for washing, of rotted posts, of ringbone and distemper" (43). In the Potter home the desires of the young are choked by the presence of the old. The past, represented by the mother, is both obstacle and threat. Stalking an old but unpredictable prey, the children act as cautious predators:

They'd lived waiting. Waiting to come together at the same lake as dogs creep out of the night to the same fire. Moving their lips when they moved them at all as hunters talk of smelling the deer. Edged close wiping plates and forks while the old lady sat in her corner. Moved lips saying: She'll live forever. And when they'd raised their eyes their mother was watching as a deer watches. (43)

This passage emphasizes the rapacity of the children, not their reasons for discontent. The emotions felt by the usurping generation have their genesis in the irrational – in jealousy, desire, and fear. And the mitigation of this irrational jealousy, desire, and fear cannot be achieved simply by the elimination of the mother. For when James kills Mrs Potter, Greta becomes the next source of fear and jealousy: she "had inherited destruction like a section surveyed and fenced ... She sat in her mother's doom as she sat in her chair" (113).

When the conflict between child and parent is played out, with youth displacing the old, the conflict is transferred to the level of brother and sister. James's desire for Lenchen poses a threat to the spinster Greta, a threat to her claim to being mistress of the household. James is presented thinking of ways of reconciling Lenchen with Greta, but he knows that Greta's hostility is unmovable:

Since the fury of the morning he'd not been able to act. He'd thrown fear as a horse balks. Then held frozen on the trail. He was afraid. He was afraid of what Greta might do ...

He had to speak. He had to say to Greta: I'm through. I'll take the girl and you can stop here or go to William. Or I'll bring her to wait on you as you waited on Ma. Or I'll bring her and you can do as you like.

He could hear the chair grating back on the boards. He could hear her voice dry in his ear: I've waited to be mistress in my own house. I never expected anything.

He could hear Greta listening at doors. He could see her counting the extra wash. Refusing to eat at table. He felt on his shoulder a weight of clay sheets. He smelt the stench of Coyote's bedhole.   (43–4)

James and Greta struggle to control family structure and to assert sexual dominion. Greta's power over James, her jealous surveillance, is truly a damp "weight of clay sheets," a tomblike snuffing out of his passion – it is a power, however, that is also associated with the unfathomable depths of Coyote's "bedhole."

From Greta's perspective, power brings its own form of entrapment. On the night that Lenchen comes to the Potter household, Greta says to the young girl, "He'll kill me too ... He'll shove me down for standing in his way" (67). Greta's fear of James, ironically, is outweighed by her jealousy of Lenchen's power over her brother, the only man in this spinster's life: as she says, "There was only James. I was never let run loose" (66). When Greta locks herself up and defiantly begins to spill kerosene into the stove to start a suicidal pyre, she thinks of Lenchen and James, and her incantatory evocation of Lenchen's death becomes a funeral song for both Lenchen's and her own self-destruction. The lack of a clear subject-referent in the sentence fragments assigned to her sets up an ambiguity that suggests that Greta is as much the lover of James as Lenchen; the ambiguity reinforces the suggestion of sexual competition:

Where's James, Greta? Tell me what you know about Lenchen and James. The girl's gone too. We must all help. We want to help you. That's why we came. Open the door, Greta. The men have gone to the barn ...

She heard Ara's voice. Tell me what you know about Lenchen.

She wanted to cry abuse through the boards. She wanted to cram the empty space with hate. She wanted her voice to shatter all memory of the girl who had stayed too long, then gone off perhaps to die in the hills. Die suffering so that James would remember the pain of her. Die young so that James would remember the sweetness of her. Die giving so that he'd live in the thought of her.   (85)

The conflicts in the Potter family arise from competition for the allegiance of a loved one. Lenchen's struggle with her mother seems less complicated but also arises out of the struggle to control desire and family structure. She, like James and Greta, is choked by the past and driven "to get away" (25):

It's enough to turn a person mad, the girl said, to have an old woman sneaking up and down the creek day in and day out. I can't stand it any longer. It's just what I was telling Ma. I've got to get away, right away from here. It's time I learned something else, anyway. I've learned all there is to learn here.   (25)

Lenchen's wish to escape is partly forced upon her, as the widow does in fact "banish" her, embarrassed at having an unmarried pregnant daughter:

From the kitchen window the Widow looked out to the hills.
    Dear God, she said, the country. Nothing but dust. Nothing but old women fishing ... The shame. A fat pig of a girl, Almighty Father. Who would want such a girl?
    I could tell you, the girl said.
    You can tell me nothing, the Widow said. Go. Go. I hear nothing. I see nothing. Men don't ask for what they've already taken.   (29)

There is a significant amount of irrational sexual jealousy in *The Double Hook*: Greta attempts to control James's sexual life; Widow Wagner, her daughter's. Ara, Greta, Lenchen, and Angel are rivals for the blessings of love, for the position of the "elect," the propagators of the community. Greta, the spinster with only her brother for company, knows what it is to be "Pitied. Scrimped. Put upon. Laughed at when no one has come for her." When she reminds Lenchen that for her "there was only James," Greta righteously upbraids her neighbour's promiscuity: "I never had two to waste and spill, like Angel Prosper" (66). Greta of course on other occasions shows how she has paid close attention to the sexual habits of those around her. Both jealously and with deliberate malice, she lists the possible forms of male infidelity in the community for Ara's edification:

If I'd married a man and gone off, there's no telling what might have happened. He might be riding round the country in a truck. Stopping and talking to women in the road. He might be leaning over the counter buying thread for somebody. He might be playing the fiddle while the pains was on me. He might be meeting the Widow's girl down in the creek bottom. He might be laying her down in the leaves.
    Ara had been looking at Greta.
    You've no right to speak that way of the girl, Ara said. You don't know.
    You don't know what I know Greta said.   (37)

Greta's speech on the inconstancy of men pricks the suspicion of Ara, who is married but childless and who also has cause to resent the pregnant Lenchen. Reminded by the innuendo of Greta, Ara confronts her own husband, William:

What's loving? she asked. Loving just makes trouble. Look at the girl Wagner, she said. She's got through loving what loving never gave me, and it's as much or more shame to her. I told Greta not to speak that way, but I know. Was Greta right, too, about your leaning over counters when you're not here. Are you looking for someone else to get children for you? Who is the father of the Wagner girl's child? Tell me, she said. William, tell me.   (75–6)

There are other instances in which conflicts within the family result from the suspicion that family allegiances are being eroded: Greta's resentment of Lenchen's seduction of James; Wagner's shame over her daughter's pregnancy; Ara's suspicion of William; and Theophil's innuendo-laden argument with Angel – "You came jumping into my bed over Felix's back," he says to Angel, "and you've got me squatting nice for another jump" (73). Even Kip is drawn into the arena of sexual jealousy and conflict when he attempts to extort favours from Lenchen in exchange for news from James (62). Only in the town is sexual jealousy not at stake, for there sex is a commodity, and the object of desire is not the fidelity of a loved one, but money.

What is the significance of these conflicts in the novel? What preoccupations do they indicate? As we begin to sort out the lines of attachment, the loved ones and the competitors for love, we see that these conflicts contribute to the irrationalization of power struggles in *The Double Hook* and to the reinforcment of Watson's romantic ideology; that the question of why the social turmoil in this world seems unresolvable is answered by examining the implied author's preoccupation with distrust, fear, betrayal, jealousy, desire, anger, and brutality – with how these surge and bubble perpetually beneath the surface of social interactions; and with how, often, disaster erupts.

According to the conventional readings of *The Double Hook*, somehow all the corrosive processes that eat away at the harmony of human relationships are, by the close of the novel, mitigated by the co-operation, charity, and pragmatic action that are necessitated by the crises in the community. One is never told that these are absolute guarantees against the resurfacing of old problems. Certainly a sense of family renewal is presented: Angel has returned to Felix; Ara has visions of a fertile land; James returns to his family; Lenchen has her baby; and the Widow Wagner appears reconciled to her daughter's condition. But can the birth of a child and the gnomic assertions of a deity mitigate the murder of a mother, the blinding of a boy, the whipping of two women – one of them pregnant – and the suicide of

Jame's sister? (And all within the time-frame of forty-eight hours!) Certainly the Widow Wagner recognizes that the child of Lenchen is born into a fallen world, and says, "I never see baby-clothes ... that I don't think how a child puts on suffering with them" (119).

Somehow, the attempts by conventional critics to make these acts of violence function only as the metaphoric pieces of an allegory contradict the authority of the implied author's voice, a voice that compels us to despair of any possibility of rationally resolving power conflicts and of achieving social harmony. All that can be hoped for in *The Double Hook* is the benevolent intervention of the gods. What the author offers is a mystery that is not framed as allegory, or "dream," as, say, Chaucer does in *The Book of the Duchess* or *The House of Fame*.

The Double Hook, like scripture, implicitly resists this questioning of its authority, or its correspondence to reality; for once we do begin to interrogate it, the novel's strategies for entrapping the reader in a world of miracles become all too apparent, and we become the heretical demystifiers of its authority. What Auerbach says of the epistemological authority of the Bible, hence, applies to *The Double Hook*:

The Bible's claim to truth is not only far more urgent than Homer's, it is tyrannical – it excludes all other claims. The world of the Scripture stories is not satisfied with claiming to be a historically true reality – it insists that it is the only real world, is destined for autocracy ... Scripture stories do not, like Homer's, court our favor, they do not flatter us that they may please us and enchant us – they seek to subject us, and if we refuse to be subjected we are rebels.

Let no one object that this goes too far, that not the stories but the religious doctrine, raises the claim to absolute authority; because the stories are not, like Homer's, simply narrated "reality." Doctrine and promise are incarnate in them and inseparable from them; for that very reason they are fraught with "background" and mysterious, containing a second, concealed meaning. In the story of Isaac, it is not only God's intervention at the beginning and the end, but even the factual and psychological elements which come between, that are mysterious, merely touched upon, fraught with background; and therefore they require subtle investigation and interpretation, they demand them. Since so much in the story is dark and incomplete, and since the reader knows that God is a hidden God, his effort to interpret it constantly finds something new to feed upon. (*Mimesis* 12)

"Authority is founded on the illusions of miracle and mystery" (195), observes Richard Sennett, commenting on Dostoyevsky's parable of the Grand Inquisitor in *The Brothers Karamazov*. The authority of *The Double Hook* is founded on the illusions of miracle and mystery. The ideology or world-view of *The Double Hook* promotes irrationality and epistemological uncertainty by scripting the reader as the recipient of an authoritative narrative voice, by immersing us in an alien landscape, by presenting transcendental spiritual events, and by making irrational familial rancour and sexual conflict the source of power struggles. However, there is a crucial rhetorical tension here between the epistemological uncertainty that is promoted in the text and the vatic aspirations and authority of the implied author. What the implied author authoritatively proposes is that the world is resistant to human understanding because of irrational human desire and the influence of immanent spiritual powers.

3 *Beautiful Losers*: Escape from Freedom

Linda Hutcheon has described *Beautiful Losers* as an early form of Canadian "postmodern metafiction: ironic, historical, and political fiction that is also about fiction, that contains within itself a first critical commentary on its own nature as narrative and as language" (*Canadian Postmodern* 27). The sophisticated intertextual references to history, to writing and reading, to the commodification of the body and the mechanistic elements in popular culture are a way of drawing the reader into an awareness of the problems of naming, translating, and the loss of a central self in modern Canada. Before noting parallels between Leonard Cohen's work and that of Rabelais, as described by Bakhtin, Hutcheon says that Cohen "implicitly posits a new role for readers: we are not simply to identify with characters, but to acknowledge our own role in co-creating the text being read. Almost like authors, readers must accept responsibility for actively participating in the constructing of the fictive worlds through words as we read" (27). Hutcheon's commentary has opened up an important angle on this imaginative work by Cohen: the reader's construction of the text.

Certainly our activity as reconstructing readers working at the site of *Beautiful Losers* is challenged by what George Dillon would describe as a personal and outrageously confrontational style. This is a hard rhetoric that does not try to persuade through polite indirection. The narrative personae are deliberately self-deprecating, extravagantly obscene, and by turns bombastic and despairing: this is a rhetoric that compels us to push back, resist, and question the values presented. Here we enter into a rhetorical transaction with the 1964 North American version of the "underground man" described by Irving Howe:

The underground man, both as a literary figure and social type, first enters European awareness in the nineteenth century. As rebel against the previously secure Enlightenment, he rejects the claims of science, the ordered world-view of the rationalists, the optimism of the radicals. He speaks in the accents of Romanticism, but a Romanticism gone sour and turned in upon itself. He is tempted neither by knowledge, like Faust, nor glory, like Julien Sorel; he is beyond temptation of any sort. The idea of ambition he regards as a derangement of ego, and idealism as the most absurd of vanities. He hopes neither to reform nor to cure the world, only to escape from beneath its pressures. For he believes – it is the one thing he believes entirely – that the world is intent upon crushing him, and he takes a spiteful pleasure in delaying its victory. That in the end it will crush him, he never doubts.   (*Decline of the New* 54)

The alienated underground man who can form allegiances with no one speaks in the various narrative voices assembled by Leonard Cohen in *Beautiful Losers*: the implied author sympathizes with these narrators, these underground men who reject rationalism and speak in the accents of a romanticism gone sour. This accent seems especially popular in twentieth-century writing, for the self-destructive voices created by Cohen in *Beautiful Losers* are not only preceded by Dostoevsky's Underground Man but are also part of the recent phenomenon of nihilistic and rebellious first-person voices created by Céline, Jean Genet, William Burroughs, and Henry Miller. Intertextually echoing these authors, the voices of the novel experiment with a decadent radicalism, a kind of directionless revolt against the truisms of political, social, and economic repression, yet also mock this radicalism: the state, the church, and capitalism are targeted for criticism, but these larger institutions are never clearly shown as the source of oppression in this psychedelic narrative collage, which ranges through mock-history, hagiography, pornography, pop-culture parody, and frenetic oration.

Beautiful Losers is obsessed with the boundaries and paradoxical entanglements of two impulses in human nature: material gratification and spiritual longing for transcendence of the material world. The chief characters both long for and fear the disappearance of divine spirit in the conjunction of earthly flesh. The unnamed narrator in book 1 is obsessed with an Iroquois saint whose destructive self-mortification is as relentless as the sexual escapades that he and his lovers stage. The narrator's best friend, identified only by the single letter "F," is presented as existing in perpetual heat, though his anxious sexual thrashings are failed attempts at connection and love. Sex becomes, paradoxically for these anti-authoritarian radicals, a means of celebrating submission, of fulfilling an urge for enslavement and the forgetting of one's identity: indeed, slavery is a consolation for the personae that Cohen presents, an escape from the unbearable responsibility of contemporary freedom.

THE VOICES OF AMBIVALENCE AND SURRENDER

The titles of the three books that make up *Beautiful Losers* alert the reader to the different contexts that frame the sections and to the different narrative strategies. Book 1, "The History of Them All," is presented in the first-person voice of a folklorist-historian. Book 2, "A Long Letter from F.," is addressed to the unnamed first narrator by F, his friend and lover, from the occupational-therapy room of a hospital. Book 3 is narrated by a detached third person. The narrator of book 3 is assigned the greatest authorial power because of his omniscient perspective. This final narrator seems to me to be allied with the implied author who sympathizes with or sanctions the utterances of the other preceding narrators – the two others are simply verbal masks, or different versions of the implied author's voice, for all the narrators display the poetic gifts, penchant for puns, and linguistic precocity of the avant-garde writer. In this analysis I will concentrate largely on the addresser-addressee relationship in the opening of book 1, since this book constitutes the largest part of the novel and sets a special precedent for the shorter books 2 and 3, though the voice of F in book 2 and the conflated voices in book 3 will occasionally be referred to.

In the opening of the first book Cohen presents the voice of a disillusioned and sardonic scholar of the "A—" Indians, a people whose "brief history is characterized by incessant defeat" (5). Cohen deliberately sets up the attitude of the narrator to one of his imagined addressees, Catherine, as ambivalent, for there are extreme shifts in the narrator's tone: he treats Catherine as a muse and a saint but also as a love object; he begins politely and decorously but then lapses into the ribald and bawdy; the religious, pastoral picture of his saint, in fact, becomes his centrefold. This is a reduction, however, that the narrator will be frightened by, for he ultimately wants Catherine to be more divine than mortal; he needs the divine to console his own disenchanted and fearful conscience.

The ambivalence of the narrator is evident in the complex layering of different addresser-addressee relations built up in the long opening first paragraph: the implied narrator, the addresser, poses his questions to an addressee whose identity he is not even sure of; he does not know *what* Catherine is, whether a fictional or historical entity: "Catherine Tekakwitha, who are you? Are you (1656–1680)? Is that enough? Are you the Iroquois virgin? Are you the Lily of the Shores of the Mohawk River?" (3) Is Catherine measurable as a mere chronological unit; is she best understood by her cultural and material status; or is she to be accorded a mythic status and to be addressed with the formal epithet "Lily of the Shores of the Mohawk River"? In the first five sentences of *Beautiful Losers* we can track the narrator moving through various footings, shifting from the flatly denotative tombstone numbers to the metaphoric flower. The movement, from the plain to the more formal levels of address, is, granted, not abrupt, but represents a calculated movement within a hierarchy of styles: this narrator represents an intellectual who moves easily in a realm of abstract distinctions and theoretical gradations. However, his training does not help him to resolve the tensions in his ambivalent and conflicting attitudes to Catherine.

The narrator's ambivalence is further exemplified in his shifts between polite requests and coarse personal deprecation. He moves from the interrogation of Catherine's identity to musing aloud on his own motives and abilities, musing at first couched in the form of a cautious request for permission: "Can I love you in my own way?" The narrator then shifts into egotistic celebration – "I am an old scholar, better looking now than when I was young" – but quickly collapses into the bitter irony of "That's what sitting on your ass does to your face" (3). He moves from the tea-room realm of politely indirect inquiry to the bawd's realm of blunt advances: "I've come after you Catherine Tekakwitha. I want to know what goes on under that rosy blanket. Do I have any right?" (3)

The narrator achieves a polite tone, suitable for addressing a saint, with such phrases of deference as "Could you," "May I say," "you must know more," and "I swear I won't mind." Such locutions indicate that the speaker might suspend his own power in order to consider the requests of the addressee: the addresser wants to maintain an image of considerate awareness. But these urbane politeness devices are mixed with outrageous improprieties. By continually mixing decorous and coarse types of address, the narrator deflates the status of his muse, Catherine, and mocks her mythical status as "Iroquois virgin, Lily of the Shores of the Mohawk River." However, this discounting of the spiritual, the narrator's thrusting of Catherine into a material world, will be cause for the narrator's lamentation when he later will act as a supplicant for divine inspiration and enslavement.

There is a self-destructive impulse in the narrator of "The History of Them All"; Cohen wants the reader to consider seriously these destructive impulses, and implicit in this desire is a paradoxical critique and celebration of the violent sensory fetishisms of the novel. It seems obvious that the narrator's attitude to the human subject, while ambiguous, flirts with a kind of Dionysian nihilism. Here the narrator's discourse reduces not only his muse but himself as well. He deliberately mocks his intellectual vocation and is given to anti-literary impulses (see Mandel, *Another Time* 128); he is weary, yet he longs for an identity, any identity, for he is so desperate that he has given up on discriminating between principles and ideology. In fact, he has given up fixed belief in exchange for the excitement of ever-changing random actions. But the price he pays for the pursuit of this excitement is a profound existential loneliness and fear. And it is this fear that transforms his discourse into a supplication and prayer for divine inspiration – to be possessed by external power, to be a slave is the consummation wished for.

Although the narrator in "The History of Them All" might be described as a stylistic exhibitionist (Ondaatje, *Leonard Cohen* 49), this exhibitionist excess signifies a deeper anxiety, a desperate attempt to hide his fear with an elaborate blanket of words. But the self-loathing and anxiety in the narrator's discourse is obvious both to us and to himself. The lonely, loveless scholar not only ridicules Saint Catherine by reducing heaven to "one of those little plastic altars that glow in the dark" but flaunts his indifference to scholarship, history, and knowledge. He has surrendered to the surface sensations of life, too tired to debate the institutionalized ideas that once elicited his hatred: "I don't even hate books any more. I've forgotten most of what I've read and, frankly, it never seemed very important to me or to the world. My friend F. used to say in his hopped-up fashion: We've got to learn to stop bravely at the surface. F. died in a padded cell" (4).

The narrator's attitude is consistent with the self-destructive trajectory of the actions of all the characters in *Beautiful Losers*: they continually cast off knowledge, traditions, and structures that provide their lives with meaning, even while fully aware of the dangers of this nihilism. Here the narrator professes an indifference to literary-historical archaeology and seems sympathetic to F's "brave" superficiality, even while knowing F's fate; yet the narrator ironically discounts the probing of the past that has unearthed his own muse, Catherine Tekakwitha. Perhaps, however, such a muse is appropriate for the narrator: she dies of self-inflicted wounds.

The self-destructive impulse in Cohen's narrator is accompanied by the extreme confusion concerning identity that a capitalist society encourages. The world offers up thousands of roles, like so many commodities, and implants a desire for the consumption of all products. This consumerism is exemplified when the narrator recalls discovering two coupons in his wife's dresser, one advertising a technique for "Slenderizing Heavy Legs" and another for improving "skinny legs" (136–7). Edith's interest in both ads fits thematically with the confusion that the narrator and the society in general exhibit about its failings: everyone feels inadequate in some way and hungers for the special commodity that will fulfil that need; but no one can pinpoint the problems, and thus each subscribes indiscriminately to all methods of "improvement."

In *Beautiful Losers* freedom of choice has been displaced by an insatiable appetite for new and surprising products and life-styles. Characters are caught up in changes in fashion and the pursuit of new sensations, the ethos of North American capitalism. This appetite is presented ambiguously by the implied author, who seems to see material desire as an inescapable condition. The implied author obsessively inserts the consumer's verb "want" into all of the character's utterances, usually in the first person past tense: "I always wanted to be loved by the Communist Party and the Mother Church. I wanted to live in a folk song like Joe Hill. I wanted to weep for the innocent people my bomb would have to maim. I wanted to thank the peasant father who fed us on the run" (24). Here the narrator wants to take on various personae; he wants a fluid, non-ideological identity: hence, he presents himself as desiring the love of all institutions, the secular and the religious, the victims and the oppressors, the opponents of his own cause and the partisans. He desires a revolutionary status that would make him into the hero of all, a messiah figure who might command allegiance from all sides among the warring groups. In his fantasies, opponents are suddenly converted into comrades, all conflict and competition neutralized. In his messianic fantasy of compelling love from his enemies he assumes the role of a mediator, infiltrates positions of power, yet comports himself with the romantic swagger of the outrageous clown hero: "I wanted to rush across America in a sealed train, the only white man who the Negroes will accept at the treaty convention. I wanted to tell an old girl friend who is appalled at my methods that revolutions do not happen on buffet tables, you can't pick and choose"(25).

Sub-section 10 of "The History of Them All" consists almost entirely of a series of "I wanted to" sentence openings: the construction is used twenty-six times. This repetition creates a sense both of uncontrolled desire and of the narrator's refusal to choose an identity or be committed to any one principle: he is unable to discriminate between the objects of desire, unable to evaluate and rank his wants, unable to distinguish among contradictory allegiances. Much of our impression of the narrator's inability to make logical distinctions comes from the seemingly non-stop use of schemes of repetition – especially anaphora. The effect of this unusual repetition of sentence openings is both to intensify the incantatory hysteria in the narrator's voice and to emphasize just how much he lacks by the intensity of how much he wants.

A deep fear of the disappearance of divine presence impels the narrator to call for divine inspiration, possession, and enslavement. The narrator's discourse, when he is acting as supplicant to God, often begins in despair and anger. This discourse is exemplified by the "I would like to accuse the Church" section of the novel, with the "I accuse the Church" (58) phrase repeated some twelve times and asyndetically stitched together with comma splices in a long run-on sentence. The anger and obscenity in the tirade barely conceal the desperation that prefaces this address. That important Cohen verb "want" appears again, this time not as a call for self-apotheosis but as an appeal to some divine power to take over the narrator and control him: "I'm tired of facts, I'm tired of speculations, I want to be consumed by unreason. I want to be swept along" (58).

Earlier, the narrator wanted "heroism" (24) and a vaguely romantic identity; now he wants to be the object of some sensational force: "I want to be consumed by unreason." Earlier the narrator desired some heroic stature as a rebel figure who fights for all underground causes, a powerful autonomous force; now he vigorously begs for enslavement, "to be swept along," to be a victim. Terrified by loneliness and silence – for silence is the absence of the spirits who can charge the bodies of men with mystical escape – he becomes the supplicant for divine recognition. The narrator begs for a sign, a relief from his spiritual loneliness and boredom: "O God, please terrify me. The two who loved me, why are they so powerless tonight?" (58).

In Beautiful Losers only the mad can have communion with the terror of God. In book 2, "A Long Letter from F.," the narrator's friend F, ex-member of Parliament and terrorist, speaks in his letter to the narrator with more confidence about the existence of God and Magic: "God is afoot. God never died. God was ruler though his funeral lengthened. Though his mourners thickened Magic never fled. Though his shrouds were hoisted the naked God did live. Though his words were twisted the naked magic thrived ... This I mean to whisper to my mind. This I mean to laugh with in my mind"(198–9).

The incantatory repetition of "God is alive. Magic is afoot" is meant to summon up belief in something marvellous, some energy that might be tapped despite the death of the "God." The limitations of the flesh are presented in a new light – flesh is spirit manifest in time: "flesh itself is Magic dancing on a clock" (199). F's rhetoric is stylistically similar to that used by the narrative voice in book 1, for it tends to use simple schemes of repetition and parallelism; the redundancy in its style is exaggerated and is immediately recognizable – repetition etches itself into memory. Moreover, this passage is spiritually affirmative rather than tragic, a celebration of the resurrection of gods and magic, a tonally ebullient and enthusiastic exhortation. But this is a consolation for F, who, according to the narrator of book 1, "died in a padded cell" (4). Here tragic elements are attached to the most affirmative impulses.

An obvious instance of this attaching of the tragic to the discourse of affirmation occurs when Cohen presents the narrator's extravagantly copious sexual tirade. The narrator drenches the reader with the noises, smells, textures, and talk of sex in a long run-on series of hyperbolic images of oral sex. The description (80–4) is outrageous, funny, but ultimately melancholy. It relates to the rhetoric of self-reduction by celebrating the nihilistic joy of losing one's identity; the narrator presents himself as joyfully consumed by his lover while consuming her. Yet this "total" connection, this torrent of words and corresponding torrent of oral sexual stimulation that the narrator luxuriates in, ends in a melancholy exhortation to a phantom of sexual desire, and it betrays the narrator's truly isolated position, his true loneliness: "thy dark lonely husband" (84). This is less of a triumphant celebration than a desperate attempt to reify the sexual experience, to freeze it and keep it from slipping into the past, to be forever immersed in its climactic moments.

When we read such sections, we become aware of the copious language that is produced, a verbal substitute for the copious fluid of sex described in the passage – indeed, Linda Hutcheon has commented on how "the novel's sexuality and even obscenity of theme and language invite us to see that here it is the flesh that is made word. In fact, without the flesh the word might never be" (*Canadian Postmodern* 28). Cohen's narrator's language is so out of control – asyndetic, unsubordinated, seriated, redundant – that its enthusiastic excess is suspect, an overcompensation for some hollow, unfulfilled part of his being. The darkness and the loneliness in the narrator's life is not mitigated through self-discovery. These can only be changed though external forces. The narrator does not find anything within himself to assuage his feelings of existential loss and his fear that the world has become intolerably banal and disenchanted. He despairs of finding a means of revivifying his spiritual life through the dead Saint Catherine:

I have been writing these true happenings for some time now. Am I any closer to Kateri Tekakwitha? The sky is very foreign. I do not think I will ever tarry with the stars. I do not think I will ever have a garland. I do not think ghosts will whisper erotic messages in my warm hair. I will never find a graceful way to carry a brown bag on a bus ride. I'll go to funerals and they won't remind me of anything. It was years and years ago that F. said: Each day you get lonelier.   (121)

The narrator in "The History of Them All" consistently uses a discourse whose aim is to surrender the self to an external power. The narrator begins by ironically deflating the power of his own muse, Catherine Tekakwitha. His own discourse reveals him searching for an identity, yet surrendering to contradictory choices that prevent him from having any kind of identity: he rages against the Church, yet he becomes a supplicant for divine intervention; and his extravagant sexual display reveals a lack of connection, his loneliness. The narrator, however, deliberately assumes positions of disadvantage to himself. What is common to all the political complaints, metaphysical lamentations, and exhortations to the gods is the intensity of the pursuit of self-immolation.

Another important function of the narrator's rhetoric is to overwhelm the reader, to flood us with enthusiasm, noise, and song; in the novel, authority is pulled down to make way for the gushing Dionysiac release of pleasure. This is the ultimate consumer world: the individuals are forever bored, forever unsatisfied, forever searching for orgasms; their ambitions are short-term, not entirely goalless but eminently selfish. For ultimately the authority of society stands in the way of the individual's appetite in a consumer world – and the fulfilment of appetite is what Cohen's characters seek. There is no time here for commitment and the rigours of ideology; the pleasure principle resists the authority of all ideology.

There is a paradox, however, in Cohen's presentation of the pursuit of the pleasure principle. Pleasure is depicted as a product of submission, of becoming the victim. In the liberal democratic state, legal authority exists to prevent the excessive use of power by one individual over others: this is liberal ideology. But liberal ideology is too restrictive for Cohen's narrators. Cohen assigns his narrators a rhetoric that attempts to control our apprehension of power by prodding us to be sympathetic to their directionless revolt, yet to witness their submis-

sion to the masochistic eroticism of being a victim of the faceless
wielders of power.

AUTHORITY IN PRIVATE AND PUBLIC LIFE: CONTRADICTIONS IN CULTURAL RADICALISM

In this analysis of the presentation of authority in *Beautiful Losers* one
can observe an underlying contradiction in the imaginary author's
version of cultural radicalism: underneath the counter-culture's apparent impulse to revolt is an attraction to enslavement. The desire for
subjugation, however, is presented as part of a complex symbiotic relationship between authority and the rebel. For these narrators, authority provides the necessary occasion for revolt; but revolt itself
exists mainly to enhance the sexual excitement of being enslaved, to
enhance the eroticism of the dramatic conflict between authority and
rebel-slave. Cohen's narrators may denounce colonization of weaker
societies, or the unfair use of power and influence by ruling classes;
but the narrators are portrayed as being seduced themselves by the
comforts of a surrender to authority and power in their private and
public lives. In their private lives, the eroticism of the surrender to
power is manifest in the form of sexual enslavement and masochism,
both of which pose as a form of sexual liberation; in their public lives
the attractiveness of the surrender to power is manifest in the form of
political obedience to a mass revolutionary movement, which poses
as a form of individualism or anarchism. In both private and public
life the individual's sense of self is eroded and destroyed, and freedom is lost.

As a narrator, F is preoccupied with various kinds of sexual experiment, experiments that often move in two directions: the first kind
moves towards a half-satiric and half-serious version of Norman O.
Brown's concept of "polymorphous perversity," a sexual attitude that
impels the seeking of sexual fulfilment not just through intercourse
but in non-genital stimulation. F humorously describes how his affair
with Edith included a special moment of sexual stimulation of her
ears; he criticizes "genital imperialism" and asserts that "All flesh can
come" (40): "Orgasms in the shoulder! Knees going off like firecrack-
ers! Hair in motion" (40). But while this seems like intentional mock-
ery of Brown's sexual ethos, there is a serious commitment to
radicalizing sexual attitudes in the novel. Each character desires all
other characters: the narrator's wife has an affair with his best friend,
F; F in turn has a homosexual affair with the narrator; the narrator
fantasizes about sex with his Iroquois saint, Catherine Tekakwitha.

The implied author never ridicules these sexual permutations but regards these as a natural condition: the ceaseless pursuit of the pleasure principle is not framed by critical perspective; desire may lead to disaster, but disaster is translated into aesthetic beauty in the eyes of the implied author and his narrators.

The pursuit of still further and further orgasmic experience leads to fatally cruel acts of masochism and sexual cruelty. Eros is hopelessly entangled with Thanatos as the narrator of book 1 remembers the pleasure of his dead wife's body: "Talking about transparent skin, Edith's throat was like that, the thinnest, softest cover. You thought a heavy shell necklace would draw blood. To kiss her there was to intrude into something private and skeletal" (32). The implication that liberated sex contains a death wish probably receives its most grotesque staging in the novel when F, in the midst of orgasm, deliberately drives his car into a cloth screen that has been painted to resemble a wall. The coupling of sex with the urge for self-destruction contradicts the ideology of sexual liberation that permeates the narrator's world. In most cases the experiments with liberated sexuality involve extreme subjugation, humiliation, and a death-wish.

AUTHORITY AND PUBLIC LIFE: THE INDIVIDUAL AND THE REVOLTING MASS

For the implied author of *Beautiful Losers*, an identifiable public authority is absent from modern North American society. And in the absence of a central authority, there is a need for a myth of repression so that the individual may allow himself to be drafted into a stimulating revolutionary movement that overtly promises the excitement of liberty but implicitly provides him with what he really most desires: membership in the mass movement.

The explicit political content of *Beautiful Losers* consists of anti-colonial sentiment, criticism directed at American involvement in Canadian cultural life and at the complicity of Canadians in the displacement of Indian culture: "French Canadian schoolbooks do not encourage respect for the Indians. Some part of the Canadian Catholic mind is not certain of the Church's victory over the Medicine Man. No wonder the forests of Quebec are mutilated and sold to America" (73). American control of the Canadian body politic is symbolically dramatized in the rape of Edith in an old mine, "owned indirectly by u.s. interests" (75). But the attitude of the narrator to the American "colonizer" is rendered more ambiguous when he describes opening a box of American fireworks, celebratory icons of the revolution, and he feels an American's nostalgia: "I wept as I unpacked the pieces, wept for the American boyhood I never had, for my invisible New England parents, for a long green lawn and an iron deer, for college romance with Zelda" (78).

The purpose of the revolutionary activity of the Quebec liberationists is presented as "the happy exercise of the arbitrary" by F, who plans to disrupt the visit of the queen by a rather unarbitrary bombing of a copper statue of Victoria. Later, F describes his urge to "hammer a beautiful colored bruise on the whole American monolith": "It is not merely because I am French that I long for an independent Quebec. It is not merely because I do not want our people to become a quaint drawing on the corner of a tourist map that I long for thick national borders ... I want to hammer a beautiful colored bruise on the whole American monolith"(235). F's "revolution" becomes an endless apocalyptic chain of retribution: "The English did to us what we did to the Indians, and the Americans did to the English what the English did to us. I demanded revenge for everyone. I saw cities burning, I saw movies falling into blackness. I saw the maize on fire. I saw the Jesuits punished. I saw the trees taking back the long-house roofs. I saw the shy deer murdering to get their dresses back. I saw the Indians punished. I saw chaos eat the gold roof of parliament" (236).

In F's vision of the revenge that all victims are accorded, even the material world takes back the substances that have been mined from it. But F's political antics are always undercut by his uncertainty, his love of the "arbitrary" nature of rebellion, an act perpetrated out of boredom. He confesses that he "never saw the Quebec revolution clearly, even at the time of [his] parliamentary disgrace. [He] simply refused to support the war, not because [he] was French, or a pacifist ... but because [he] was tired" (205).

Even the most explicit staging of a public revolt against authority, the mobilization of the the masses in book 3, contains an undercurrent of the desire for enslavement. A new character, who represents both F and the narrator of book 1, descends from a tree-house; this identityless character is recognized as an old separatist agitator, and he evokes a sense of revolutionary camaraderie amongst a crowd of onlookers in a Montreal street, who eventually work themselves up into a revolutionary fervour. At the same time, the voice of the implied author explicitly emerges as the voice of narration; this voice treats the magical transformation of the masses into a revolutionary body with utter sympathy: "For the first time in their lives, twenty men experienced the delicious certainty that they were at the very centre of action, no matter which side. A cry of happiness escaped from each man as he closed in on his object. Already an accumulation of tangled sirens had provoked the strolling mob like an orchestra at a bull fight. It was the first night of spring, the streets belong to the People!" (302–3) But the implied author here cannot help showing that enslavement is connected somehow to this celebration of liberty. The instigator of the revolution turns out to be an insubstantial American pop image, as the amorphous identity of the persona metamorphoses into a movie-screen image of Ray Charles: the "revolutionary terrorist" becomes the popular entertainer, the one who sings "Somebody said lift that bale" in the opening epigraph, a black song of slavery and tragic resignation from the classic American musical *Showboat*.

Wielding a self-critical rhetoric, a discourse that exposes to the reader the inadequacies, failings, and weaknesses of the narrator's thinking, the implied author of *Beautiful Losers* assumes voices that immediately justify the book's title. The reader is introduced at the outset to a loser, a historian-writer obsessed with historical losers, whose "brief history is characterized by incessant defeat." Assigned a rhetoric that attempts to be anti-authoritarian in tone, by highlighting the marginality of the addresser, the narrator's discourse really reveals his loneliness and shows how ripe he is to become the object of a powerful external authority: lamentation turns into an exhortation to the gods.

Cohen's novel reflects various assumptions concerning aesthetics, politics, and human nature. In the aesthetic dimension the implied author assumes that a collage of voices, personal therapy in the form of confessional monologue, the juxtapositions of images from pop culture, and jump-cut disjunctions are adequate forms for his message, and that the pre-positioned readership will accept these techniques; that his art can sustain a paradoxical self-parodying or anti-art impulse; and that the receptive pre-positioned reader is a liberal with some American sixties counter-culture sympathies, or at least some understanding of the hipster ironies and popular jokes of the counter-culture. In the political dimension Cohen's implied author assumes that the truisms about authoritarian institutions in North American culture are valid: that the Catholic church is responsible for sexual oppression and neuroses; that this sexual oppression is somehow paralleled by the political colonization of Canada, and specifically Quebec, by an American technological ethos; that radicalizing sexual behaviour is a suitable response.

In the metaphysical dimension Cohen's implied author assumes that there is a spiritual world that is in conflict with Western technologism but in harmony with the "Indian" way of being; that the main problem in human nature is the reconciling of the spiritual and sexual drives; that human beings are essentially "infected" with pathological madness, perversity, and a drive to self-immolation; that the important character-types that the writer should explore are the sexually and spiritually obsessed persons, the self-loathing artists.

In *Beautiful Losers* Cohen seems to criticize cultural imperialism by gathering some commonplace observations of the injustices perpetrated by the English against the French, the French against the Indians, the Americans against the English; yet the implied author glorifies the submission of the victim by making surrender into a celebrated aesthetic experience. The implied author never intrudes in order to criticize the suicidal impulses in the characters he depicts nor to distance his own commitments and interests from them. The private and public lives of his characters are shot through with the desire for enslavement, an enslavement that is eroticized by struggle but is not meant to be overthrown. The paradox of the mentality sanctioned by the implied author is strikingly similar to an aspect of modernism remarked upon by Irving Howe: "Modernism consists in a revolt against the prevalent style, an unyielding rage against the official order ... [but] modernism must always struggle but never quite triumph, and then, after a time, must struggle in order not to triumph" (quoted in Sennett, *Authority* 50). While Cohen attempts to support a counter-cultural ethos, he actually portrays the self-destructive impulse of a decadent counter-culture that has begun to struggle in order not to triumph.

4 *The New Ancestors*:
Politics and Private Life

One of the major implications of Dave Godfrey's *The New Ancestors* is that the individual's private life is richer, more complex, and more full of redeeming moments than can be encompassed by the accounts of a public institution. This experimental novel – difficult, erudite, and epic in scope – explores the relationship between the individual and social forces by presenting the viewpoints of different characters who are involved in the political life of "Lost Coast," a fictional African state that is meant to resemble Ghana of the sixties. Godfrey makes us work hard as readers to reconstruct the details of West African party alliances and policies out of the highly fragmented narrative. The internal consciousness of various characters – especially Michael Burdener and Ama Awotchi Burdener – and their private symbols, introspections, and dreams are presented in detail by the implied author, resulting in digressions that disturb the clear and precise delineation of the character's political commitments. The personal, informal, and direct footings that are constructed by the Michael and Ama points of view create a persuasive and compelling authority for their positions as characters and compel a reader's sympathy and acceptance.

There are two narrative tactics that Godfrey employs here: on the one hand, he submerges the voice of the novel's originary consciousness or implied author by presenting first-person narrators in the Michael ("The London Notebook") and Ama ("A Child of Delicacy") sections of the novel, a tactic that compels us to read their discourses as unmediated authentic confessions, though not entirely reliable, as if these were culled from diary or journal entries. The Ama section also contains the further complication of a switching of footings between first- and third-person voices. On the other hand, Godfrey subtly inserts an intervening authoritative and impersonal footing, an omniscient voice, in the prologue, in the third section focusing on First Samuels' "Freedom People's Party," and in the surreal fourth section, which contains different versions of Rusk's counter-revolutionary activities in Mali, "In the Fifth City."

In the Michael and Ama sections the identified personal narrator focuses on family relations and on individual psychology: the strategy of the implied author is to place the reader on a footing of solidarity and intimacy with the individual narrator – Michael or Ama. Here the narrator's view might be called phenomenological, for it is designed to provide the reader with the perceptions of a character through stream-of-consciousness techniques. In the other sections, including the prologue, which use an intervening omniscient voice, the narrative focuses on events that have a national or international political scope: the routines of foreign diplomats, the activities of counter-revolutionaries, the assassination of suspected CIA agents. The narrative voice in these sections, impersonal, distant, authoritative, anonymous, and therefore inscrutable, attempts to lead the reader, often through irony, to a detached, objective understanding of social and historical events. In these cases the implied author presents an authoritative footing, that of an omniscient ethical adviser.

These two tactics, the concealing of the author behind the mask of a first-person narrator and the explicit revealing of an author who subtly comments on characters in the third-person voice, roughly correspond to liberal and Marxist attitudes to the presentation of character in literature. That Godfrey uses both tactics attests to his ambition to create a polyphonic discourse that yokes together different world-views and attitudes to human nature. Christopher Butler, in *Interpretation, Deconstruction, and Ideology,* has commented on the difference between liberal and Marxist attitudes to character, and describes W.J. Harvey's *Character and the Novel* (1965) as representative of the liberal position, in which "moral decisions may take place in some inner free forum of the mind" (124) and characters are thus depicted free to decide their fates, free from the constraints of ideology. Butler cites Terry Eagleton's essay on George Eliot in *Criticism and Ideology* as exemplifying the Marxist position that "the individual has to be seen as representative of forces within society which transcend him or her, and of which he may not even be wholly conscious" (126).

Godfrey's novel encourages the reader, especially in the sections employing the concealed authorial voice, to empathize with the emotional experiences of the individual, but he also pressures the reader to temper this sympathy, especially in the sections employing explicit authorial intervention, with an understanding of the social forces and political pressures that can dwarf, or reduce in importance, the private life of the individual. By using these two narrative tactics, Godfrey is able to link together the liberal and Marxist beliefs about character, and by so doing begins to transcend the disagreement between them. Godfrey's writing seeks political orientation by attempting to show that individual will and historical determinism operate simultaneously.

Underlying Godfrey's discourse is an ethical imperative. His pluralism not only seeks to make diversity known, to present Africa as "authentically" as a Caucasian educated in North America can, but is also shot through with indignation. In *The New Ancestors* ideology is dealt with critically and cynically: Godfrey assumes that power corrupts politics; politics means dirty politics. The contemporary reader knows the kinds of political events that Godfrey presents as the commonplaces of the daily news: failed coups, assassinations, nationalism, racism, terrorism, political imprisonment and torture, the deportation of the expatriate. Godfrey never sentimentalizes political struggle.

AUTHORITY AND ANCESTRY

Authority in *The New Ancestors* emerges in national and family settings and is most obviously presented through the interplay between feelings of allegiance and feelings of contention: between the pull to obey and support the authority of the president of Lost Coast, Kofi Kruman, and the push to rebel against the quasi-socialist leader. The dynamic of attraction to and repulsion by authority is presented in the personal relationships of various characters, relationships that are often identified with the "ancestry" theme suggested by the novel's title. Godfrey often depicts the family – the power of father figures and the influence of mothers (see Robert Margeson, "Preliminary Investigation," on the Ashanti matrilineal family). He also explores the implications of racial heritage and origin and the consequences of interracial marriage, or the mixing of ancestral blood-lines: Michael Burdener as a schoolteacher combines biology and politics in his teaching and his marriage to Ama Awotchi, a native of Lost Coast. The tensions in this marriage seem to embody Godfrey's view of the larger international tensions between the Westerner who wants to spur on the radical socialization and detribalization of Africa and the African who needs more desperately a stable, peaceful, and loving national environment.

There are various levels of authority in *The New Ancestors*: Kofi Kruman, the egotist dictator president, and Gamaliel Harding, party chief of propaganda, control the state of Lost Coast. In the chain of power descending from them are further hierarchies: Gamaliel Harding wields power as a father trying to mould his delinquent son into a proper socialist soldier of the state; Michael Burdener, as a left-leaning dabbler in African politics, tries to plant a spirit of anti-colonialism in the schoolgirls at the teacher's college while teaching socio-biology and evolution. Burdener is also husband to Ama, but he cannot seem to operate outside the authority role of teacher. He is first aligned with the Kofi Kruman government, extolling the virtues of the president's ideology to his pupils, but he eventually falls into partnership with First Samuels in the attempt to undermine the Freedom People's Party.

Along with those who wield power and hold authority there are the rebels, the insurgents, or the double agents. The most significant is First Samuels, who plans to lead a Maoist-inspired guerrilla war against the government of Kofi Kruman. First Samuels is able to entice the son of Gamaliel Harding, Kwame Bird Lady Day, into joining the insurgents. The son leaves his family to fight against his own father and Kruman. Another significant "rebel" against authority is, of course, Ama: as a Lost Coast woman who marries the Englishman Burdener, she claims through marriage a set of "new ancestors." Ama rejects the heritage of Lost Coast first by becoming the mistress of Kruman and then by marrying Burdener.

These rebels are either deported, seduced back into serving the state, arrested, or executed. The attempts to control ancestry and political allegiances are mainly thwarted by the larger power of President Kruman or by irrational personal passions. The ancestral motif is linked to political rebellion and tribal alienation, and the radicals who oppose President Kruman are all alienated in some way from the ancestral positions that are respected in Lost Coast. The "displaced" ancestor is represented by the party rebel First Samuels, whose quasi-Maoist philosophy seems to have roots in his position as an alienated Nigerian in a foreign country rather than in compelling ideological principles.

Recurring ancestral and racial conflicts form an implied authorial evaluation of the urgency of certain types of social problems: the important social-bonding problems are international, interracial, and are related to our sense of the "tribe." Indeed, Godfrey's very style of narration attempts to overcome the provinciality of this tribalism. The conspicuous uses of multiple points of view and a retrospective narrative structure not only relate to an attempt to transcend the liberal-

Marxist disagreement concerning individual will and historical determinism, but also reflect the implied author's belief in historical reassessment and in the need for the observers of the individual and society to readjust their vision of the world continually in order to accommodate new information. As we become familiar with the various points of view in each section, we can reinterpret the information we receive in the prologue, perhaps even discount it: understanding the world of *The New Ancestors* is a process of re-evaluating and reinterpreting past information. Different points of view, hence, compel the reader to engage in a process of interpretation that attempts to get around the problem of cultural provincialism.

Godfrey's writing style is also designed to overcome cultural provincialism. His style is marked by an abundance of multicultural signs, from the juxtaposition of epigraphs on the title-page (one epigraph from the seventeenth-century English essayist Thomas Browne and one from the proverbs of the Akan people of Africa) to the special icons that mark the title-pages of separate sections, to the maps of Africa provided at the beginning of the book. The implied author's knowledge spans different cultures and different languages: Akan proverbs, Latin tags, and excerpts from European, African, and Oriental thought are provided, often untranslated. Our imagined author's display of multicultural erudition indicates a commitment to preserving indigenous expression and accepting cultural differences. At the same time, Godfrey prompts the reader into a self-conscious relationship with the text: to seek translations of the foreign material, or to accept one's inability to "know" the foreign signs. (In fact, in "A Note on the Missing Glossary" appended to the 1972 paperback reprint of the novel, Godfrey gives three reasons why he did not provide translations of African words: the publisher's unhappiness with the length of the book; the desire to have "the non-African reader in some way ... experience those moments of stark incomprehension which hit even the most open-minded travellers to Africa"; and the need to point out to Western scholars "the clear gaps not only in their knowledge of African cultures but in the libraries they have helped form.")

IRONY AND SHIFTING FOOTINGS IN THE "PROLOGUE," "FREEDOM PEOPLE'S PARTY," AND "IN THE FIFTH CITY"

I want to turn at this point to an examination of the narrative footings that are used to script an ironic judgment of certain characters. The prologue not only promotes an objective, rationally detached point of view by aligning the reader with the values of Geoffrey Firebank and Hastings Ayitteh; it also ironically criticizes such values. In its fourteen pages we are introduced to over a dozen characters, including Geoffrey Firebank, Michael Burdener, Hastings Ayitteh, Richard Bewsher, Rod Rusk, President Kruman, First Samuels, Kwame Harding, Gamaliel Harding, and Ama. This assembly of players is made cohesive by the perspectives of two characters who cease to have any further importance in the development of the plot after the prologue: Geoffrey Firebank and Hastings Ayitteh. Firebank and Ayitteh are bored British Council employees, haughtily more refined than the absurd political circus outside their office walls, but they are also subjected to the gentle irony of the implied author. Godfrey maintains a delicate balance between criticism and sympathy for the two, but because of the implied author's interventions, we are never as deeply immersed in their world as we are in the experiences of Michael and Ama in their sections. The flavour of the prologue, more so than that of any other section, is comic and ironic.

The prologue begins the juxtaposition of various points of view – in this case, Firebank's and Ayitteh's – that will constitute Godfrey's method throughout *The New Ancestors*. The chronological arrangement also sets up the suspension of historical explanation and pushes the reader into a retrospective process: the prologue presents the conclusion to dramatic conflicts that are chronologically at the end of the novel's plot; subsequent chapters are a retracing, from the points of view of different characters, of the fragments of past history that led up to the events presented in the prologue – the deportation of the Englishman Michael Burdener, the arrest of First Samuels, the murder of Gamaliel Harding, the love affair of some unidentified girl of the Lost Coast, the disappearance of the American Rodney Rusk and of Gamaliel Harding's son, Kwame. These tantalizingly incomplete reports and the large assembly of names attain significance for the reader only in retrospect.

Of course the tantalizingly incomplete aspect of the prologue not only enforces a process of retrospection but also facilitates the ironic treatment of Geoffrey Firebank, the "British Council Man in Silla" (1), who is presented as one of the apparent controlling points of view for the first part of the prologue. His irritated superciliousness about the problems that a representative of the British Council must deal with sets the dominant tone. And because Firebank is not really interested in the political events in Silla, the history of the conflicts presented in the prologue is incomplete: in fact, he mails back to England a package of Burdener's writing, the "London Notebook" that the *reader* opens after the prologue. Our participation in the construction of the text is thus foregrounded as we become conscious of turning the pages not only of an imaginative work but of a "notebook" as well, a technique that dates well back to the early history of the novel as a fictionalized journal or piece of imaginative life-writing.

In introducing Firebank the narrator moves from relaying Firebank's internal thoughts to an apparently straightforward physical description of him; but the tone becomes increasingly ironic. The narrator begins with the neutral measurements "extremely tall" and "well over six feet"; this seemingly positive size is translated into awkwardness, as the description caricatures him as thick-headed, with his shoulders "grown almost into his neck," an inhuman "neck-head," and his face tiredly hovering over his desk "as though he were an elderly eagle" (2). The narrator's apparently neutral commentary rapidly turns into a satirical portrait of the British Council man as less cultivated and enlightened than he imagines himself to be. He is the liberal capitalist who has rationally analysed the future of the Communist-run Lost Coast – yet he is portrayed as insensitive and coarse.

There are instances when Firebank's cynicism is seemingly unchecked by the implied author's interests. Godfrey adjusts his tone, for example, when he wants the reader to approve of Firebank's attitude to the president of Lost Coast. Firebank's sniggering contempt for the dictator is provided without obvious undercutting authorial commentary when he is presented travelling to the airport to meet his superior, Richard Bewsher, and to question Burdener on his deportation via Alitalia. He warns his driver to steer around the president's palace, where Kruman is displaying his soldiers:

"The airport, Ali," he said. "Oh, and go around the President's palace someway. They'll be marching now. A beautiful spectacle, but we'll watch it some other day."
    A complete nuisance, actually. If the President had to have his Honour Guard march in front of Flagstaff House at noon, he ought to build a square in front, so they shouldn't block the main road to the airport. Dictators had recurrent similarities. Firebank could imagine John Milton planning just that sort of show for Cromwell. Bright red uniforms and dogmatic souls. Bewsher said that the Guard was trained by the Russians.   (4–5)

Firebank is, by these kinds of observations and this type of ironic distancing, separated from the essential politics of Lost Coast. He is able to dismiss the president's parade as a mere "nuisance" and to compare the African dictator to a British "Cromwell." We later learn that the wit of the comparison is valid, given the president's penchant for theatrical costume and his view of himself as the "Redeemer." But Firebank is presented as more concerned with the inconvenience that the marching troops will present to traffic than the fact that the guards are trained by the Russians. For Firebank, that which is politically meaningful is ignored, while the trivial is overemphasized.

But Godfrey neither supports Firebank entirely nor completely dismisses his observations. In fact, Firebank's ironic attitude to the pompous display of the president is shown to reflect his healthy nose for truth – he is the sceptic, the man who must sort through the news of Lost Coast and find the least questionable lies in order to piece together a picture of the country that will enable him to get on with the pragmatic business of the British Council. Firebank's readings of various Lost Coast newspapers (5–7), represented in fragmented sentences that attempt to capture the units of meaning that he processes as he scans the newspapers, alert the reader to the stew of half-truths and ideological propaganda that Firebank must continually sift through in order to make sense of Lost Coast life. In the light of these conditions, Firebank's scepticism and irony become more sympathetic, attitudes necessary for survival.

Firebank is presented reading of the capture of First Samuels in the local papers. The *Lost Coast Mirror* is characterized as a gossip sheet; it emphasizes the "as yet unidentified Lost Coastian girl [who] had been the cause of the quarrel and the violent murder" (5). Firebank dismisses the views of this paper, though the reader in subsequent chapters will discover that a woman – or women, and love interests – do indeed influence the political decisions and political life of various men: Ama in Burdener's and the president's life; Norah in First Samuels'; Donaldo, in an indirect way, in Rusk's. The *Black Evening Star* is the ultra-socialist, anti-American paper; it, of course, begins by suggesting that some CIA plot is responsible for the "murder" and that an American soldier named "Rusk," and one Kwame Harding, were involved in an anti-government plot. We later learn that First Samuels murdered Gamaliel Harding, that First Samuels is a Nigerian who has been alienated from the Communist party of Lost Coast, and that Rusk is the one described as "the CIA resident in Lagos." We also later learn that Gamaliel Harding wrote a propaganda column in support of President Kruman for the *Black Evening Star*. In a subsequent chapter we are told of the defection of Gamaliel's son, Kwame Harding, to the anti-Kruman rebels, and the killing of Richard Rusk.

Firebank's British liberal bias is reflected in his enthusiasm for the *Agada Times*, which "in deferrence to its more famous namesakes, attempted restraint and truthfulness" (6). Firebank, appropriately, likes the discreet government criticism in the paper, the liberal attitude of protection for the Nigerian immigrants in Lost Coast, and its proposal of economic solutions to political problems: "a well-managed economy would provide jobs not only for most Lost Coastians but also for a reasonable number of such aliens" (6). Unlike the *Black Evening Star*, the *Times* "relegated mention of Rusk and Burdener to the end of an inside column" (7).

But Firebank's self-satisfied sense of superiority to the supposed lies disseminated by the gossip press and the far left is shown to be limited: even the sensationalist papers' reports contain some small elements of truth that Firebank is unable to understand. He fancies himself and "his position in independent Africa as somewhat analogous to that of a first century Greek expatriate, spreading his ideas and wisdom not in Rome but in some distant province": "Such relative examples of rationality as *The Agada Times* occasionally provided gave his spirits a lift" (7). But Firebank is not true to his supposed heritage of rationalism: the murky areas of political life, the unanswered questions that the reader must pose – Why is Burdener being deported? Who was murdered? Who is First Samuels? Was he the murderer, and what was his motive? Who is Rusk, and Kwame Harding, and who was the woman involved in the murder? – all these questions are left unanswered by Firebank, who never probes into the gaps in the descriptions of these conflicts. They are simply nuisances to him, like the president's parade. In fact, when he has the opportunity to sift through Burdener's personal notes and journals, instead of obeying his superior's request to find out as much as possible about Burdener, Firebank simply sends the material back to Burdener's address in England. He encounters much information concerning a group of characters who will be seen to be closely related in subsequent chapters: Burdener, First Samuels, Gamaliel Harding, Kwame, and Rusk are far more connected than he can imagine.

After Firebank's dismissal of the Lost Coast papers and his support of the *Times*, we are introduced to a new, native perspective on events, and the conflicts are at least made clearer, the participants described in more detail. Mr Hastings Ayitteh, Firebank's office assistant, identifies the murderer, First Samuels, and the victim, Gamaliel Harding. He notes their reputations in Lost Coast, and he assesses the characters of both men; however, the omniscient narrator again intervenes and treats the "close personal knowledge" of Ayitteh ironically:

Mr. Hastings Ayitteh, moving slowly and serenely among the wisdom entrapped in the periodicals and reference books of the Silla Reading Room of the British Council, his brow cooled by the sultry air stirred about by two white, overhead fans, meditated thus on the death of his countryman.

As for the fugitive, First Samuels, it was well known what position his family held in Silla. Riffraff convert Methodists from one of the northern bush tribes. Not of the Scottish-originated Church, but of some outcast American variety, with a negro preacher, a mulatto but an ugly man ... What could the son of such an upbringing in Silla become, except a Party thug and then a refugee and now probably a Party murderer. Hastings was certain the Party had murdered Gamaliel.   (10)

The narrator's ironic treatment of Ayitteh allows for the self-exposure of his pettiness. Ayitteh thinks of events in hyperbolic noun phrases: "wild justice," "revenge inescapable," "blasphemous and communistic ways" (10). More markedly ironic is the language of the long sentence that makes up the first paragraph above, describing the pompous Ayitteh "moving slowly and serenely" in the reading room and "meditat[ing] on the death of his countryman." The reading-room setting itself provides an ironic backdrop to Ayitteh's "personal" knowledge of these events. The narrator shifts abruptly from the leisurely suspended sentence and the pompously stuffy atmosphere of the reading room to a series of petty outbursts against "riffraff."

Hastings Ayitteh also introduces the character Ama Awotchi Burdener: we do not know at this point that she is Michael's estranged wife, but we learn that she *is* related to the dead Gamaliel Harding: "It would be a long process to welcome her back into the family; there were many ruptures and hurt prides. She had not attended Gamaliel's funeral service" (12). Ama's introduction is important because it completes the introduction of all the characters whose consciousnesses will be the central points of view in the next five sections of the novel: Michael Burdener in "The London Notebook"; Ama Awotchi Burdener in "A Child of Delicacy"; First Samuels in "Freedom People's Party"; Rusk in "In the Fifth City"; and Michael again in the "Agada Notebook" concluding section.

First Samuels and Rod Rusk are presented far less sympathetically than Michael Burdener or Ama: there is no sentimental love interest in their lives (even First Samuels' relationship with Norah is pointedly anti-romantic); they are less pitiable, and are subject to the criticism of the implied author who narrates their sections or to the criticisms of other characters. First Samuels, a quasi-Maoist revolutionary who schemes the overthrow of Kruman and imagines himself leading Lost Coast to its own "great leap forward" (see 181, 211, 222), is never presented as fully from the "inside" as Michael and Ama are: chronologically, his section begins after his arrest for planning the bombing of the Kruba dam, "Job 600," and for the murder of Gamaliel Harding, then shifts back in time to trace some significant phases of his development. However, he is introduced at the beginning of the "Freedom People's Party" section from the point of view of Father Skelly, the head of Bishop Adisa school, where First Samuels attained notoriety for embezzling money from his own family. Skelly sees the young Nigerian outlaw as a mere imitation of the corrupt Kruman and believes "they can't build jails fast enough to keep up with them, because they are nothing but imitations of Kruman himself. They see just how he gathered in the wealth – by saying us and doing I – and they follow him, they imitate him, they are him" (165–6).

Godfrey's implied author introduces a distasteful element of intolerance and conceit in First Samuels' character. When he is shown visiting a workers' organization, he is depicted as perceiving both the setting and the people with contempt:

He spent a long time locking up the car. Glancing up at the garish concrete buildings of the Technical Workers' Co-op with the red and black paint flaking off in the dim light. In the dim light the green mould was clearly visible in the concrete drains ...

Inside, he felt surrounded by clerkmen. Indians. Children of mixed-marriages. Dirty Peace Corps people. Burdener was probably here, sniffing around. It was what he raged against, but where else did he spend all his time? Pure feelings of disgust circled within him. Biney was right, old Alegba had more revolution in him than these misfits. They seemed willing to mix with anyone, to accept anything, to live in any filth.

But he was one of them, really, if they could see it. Hastings Awotchwi would have pushed him down here for sure. And he had given up more than they had even dreamed of doing. Yet why did they move and drink and argue at a speed he couldn't really adjust to nor understand ... Real Maoism would cure them, he knew. Real confrontations.   (210–11)

The implied author's judgment of Rod Rusk is even more severe. Rusk's section, "In the Fifth City," is the most exotically violent, and the most disjointed in narrative terms. The intrigue of illegal mercenary activity, not its goals and principles, is emphasized, and the narrator therefore is primarily interested in creating a mysterious series of impressions, a smoky climate of suspense. For example, he emphasizes the desert atmosphere of Mali, with its ominously masked Arab Tuaregs who rumble off on horseback into the dark after killing their enemy; or the Conradian parallels in the river journey that Rusk and his mercenary aides embark on; the cold-war espionage theatrics of interrogation and torture that the American Rusk is plunged into when captured by the Soviet bloc soldier Chelmiak; or the exotically decadent combination of sexual desire and torture, reminiscent of Lawrence Durrell, in the sequences where Donaldo Pedro, wife of the Portuguese consul, witnesses one of the many versions of Rusk's death.

Rusk is never assigned the kinds of confessional opportunities that

Ama and Michael are. Indeed, the author-narrator perhaps evaluates this character more harshly than any other: "For there is something truthfully if indefinably American about him: an assurance, a willingness to smile, a lust after quantification, a competitive strength, a simple purity, a repetition of certain key phrases and ideas in all situations, a limited understanding of the ignobly tragic, a solidness to the body, a taste for steak, a shallowness of comprehension of other modes of social interaction than his own"(316–17).

When presenting Rusk, Godfrey's implied author repeatedly dramatizes his "shallowness of comprehension of other modes of social interaction than his own." His approach in this section is therefore similar to that used in the prologue. By subjecting the perspectives of characters like Rusk, Firebank, Hastings Ayitteh, and First Samuels to ironic exposure, he permits his readers to join in the ironic resistance to their shallowness: these four lack the compelling self-consciousness that other characters seem to have. They live almost exclusively in a world of public issues, social theories, and policies, cut off, perhaps out of choice, from emotional life, and lacking any deep understanding of the psychological bonds behind the political scandals that surrounded them. The implied author's own political bias is reflected in his ironic interventions; he emphasizes the deficiencies in public performers like First Samuels and sets up sympathy for the private discourses of more introspective individuals like Michael and Ama.

PERSONAL FOOTINGS AND PATHOS IN "THE LONDON NOTEBOOK" AND "A CHILD OF DELICACY"

The presentation of the interior consciousness of Michael and Ama immediately lends a stamp of authenticity to their discourse: they may not display more convincing political and social insights into Lost Coast life than do Firebank, Ayitteh, First Samuels, or Rusk, but the appearance of direct, unmediated confession puts them on a personal, informal, and direct footing with the reader. Even though the reliability of the Michael and Ama narrators is questionable, their discourse is emotionally persuasive.

"The London Notebook" is a hypothetical reading of the journals and notes that Geoffrey Firebank sent to England after Burdener's deportation. In this section Michael's speech shifts continually between the spontaneous and the formulaic. Burdener's discourse often *appears* to be craftless and confessional – "I begin to sound like a lonely man to you?" (20) – yet he also speaks in rhetorical commonplaces and epigrams: "If authority is unjust, revenge takes the helm" (21);

"Cynicism and craft are not enough; knowledge must be added" (61). "Don't reveal secrets without an advantage gained: That is my second rule. *Homo homini lupus*" (16), says Burdener, a quotation that also appears in Freud's *Civilization and Its Discontents*, a tag from Plautus meaning "Man is wolf to man." Many of the African politicians, like Gamaliel Harding, utter gnomic Akan proverbs, and Michael's own proverbial expressions show him recalling Western commonplaces and adapting these for the arena of political speech around him.

The tone of Michael's discourse is cynical. He is preoccupied with his alienation from both England and Africa, his insecurity as a father, and his "failed revenges for humiliation" (50). His interactions with Gamaliel Harding show that the Englishman is aching to defeat his opponent; he seeks to triumph over his brother-in-law, yet he fears this party-worker's power. He knows that Gamaliel Harding's family regards him as an object of scorn, a scapegoat, and his alienation from his African relations deepens his sense of alienation: "I know how I am spoken of, perhaps that is the first thing to set clear: in whispers, in analysis, and in loud goatish laughter. *Pharmakos. Basa-basa*" (16).

Part of Godfrey's implied author's strategy in presenting Michael's exclusion from the family is to show him as a problematic link between social history and individual feeling. Michael is linked to a new family through his marriage to Ama, a new line of "ancestors." But the family union is uneasy: when Burdener is presented trying to comfort his ill son, Cricket, the young child calls for the care of his mother instead, inflicting upon Michael as father "the hurt of the exclusion despite all his rationality" (29). And Burdener's confession of his pain at this point makes his problem more authentic than the political problems facing First Samuels or Rusk.

The implied author purposely returns to the "ancestors" theme by having Michael narrate various father-son conflicts. The son's rejection of the father is a motif that is repeated in a different context when Michael, acting in his capacity as schoolmaster, informs his brother-in-law, Gamaliel Harding, of his son's delinquent behaviour at Bishop Adisa school. The subsequent breakdown of the relationship between Gamaliel and Kwame Harding allows Burdener to wreak revenge on Gamaliel. Burdener has been publicly humiliated by Gamaliel – beaten and accused of carrying venereal disease by Gamaliel's mentally ill mother. And Gamaliel is especially cruel to his own son, forcing him to memorize revolutionary catechisms and punishing his errors with an antelope-hide whip.

Michael's encounters with Gamaliel and discussions of Kwame's "impregnations and hashish," and Gamaliel's need to make "revolutionists of the merely unruly" (23), draw together some of Michael's power preoccupations. He is alienated from a secure "ancestry" or family group because of his foreign status in Africa; the conflict between father and son is related to the problem of ideological indoctrination, and becomes apparent when Michael meets with Gamaliel to discuss Kwame's future at school. Gamaliel is an aide to the president, and becomes a dangerous opponent when Michael shifts his allegiances to First Samuels and the rebels.

Harding is the unpredictable ideological spokesman for the president of Lost Coast. He attempts to tyrannize many of those around him: his brother-in-law Michael; his sister Ama; his son Kwame. Burdener himself assists Gamaliel in one instance in interrogating Kwame. When the boy stumbles in trying to describe the "primary purpose of neocolonialists in Africa," Gamaliel punishes him with a cruel whipping. The whipping is described in language that metaphorically anticipates the murder of Gamaliel by First Samuels, who attacks him in a crowded rally with a studded ball:

Facing his father, his back still to me, Kwame Bird Lady Day shivers into a mock stupidity, hearing my voice at his back.

"That is merely the first of the catechism. What any small boy should know. When it comes to the breakdown of the economic, few are more foolish than you. You will never reach the point at which the wise can question the Redeemer."

All the marks of manhood approached shimmer in his body as he turns to me. A gangling thinness. A fear of lacking sufficient pride.

"What is the primary purpose of neocolonialists in Africa?"

"Division."

Then he stumbles. The ball of learning hits a corner and bounces off erratically, and, as the mind spins to catch it, he trips, the ball speeds up again, strikes him, disappears into the sky, strikes him again from behind and dribbles into inaction before he can catch it. "Multiplication," he smiles out weakly.

Gamaliel's fist, holding the short whip of antelope hide thongs, crashes into his son's shoulder blades. (81)

What is the attitude of the implied author to this struggle? Does it expose Burdener's complicity in the subjugation of the son? We have already noted Burdener's uneasy relationship with his own children. And there are various references to the breakdown of the family, or the corruption of ancestral blood-lines: various disease images are associated with the corruption of the family. Michael is accused of having venereal disease by Harding's mother (Michael's mother-in-law). Gamaliel actually abets Michael's public humiliation, and this provokes Burdener to steal the medical file on Delicacy Harding –

"knowledge is necessary for directed evil" (68); with the medical file on Delicacy, Burdener boasts that "I will destroy Gamaliel and have him help me destroy this now fraudulent revolution, this capitalistic Redeemer, this scourge of Africa" (69). And, one might add, the line of ancestors who have become a threat to Burdener rather than a comfort.

Burdener's motive for his shift of allegiance is revenge: revenge for the humiliation he suffers at the hands of Delicacy, for the alienation of himself and Ama from their family foundation, for the racist rejection of Michael by Delicacy, for the malign power exerted by Gamaliel over Michael's marriage. When Burdener plans his revenge, he envisages manipulating Kwame, for as an ideological strategist he is well aware of the contradiction that exists between the imperialist injustice of the father-son relationship and the supposedly socialist state: the "capitalist" president will be punished by the young rebels who seek their own share of capitalist affluence (82). Michael is preoccupied with his role as a scapegoat, with his brother-in-law Harding, his alienation from his son, his need for revenge – the whole of his section sets up *reasons* for vengeance: the thrust is Michael's sense of self-righteousness. In contrast, Ama's section is much more revisionary, and often takes the form of a dialogue with her memories, with the voices of friends and lovers.

The world of "The London Notebook" is filled with hate, humiliation, and the pain of unfulfilled desire for vengeance. This is the world of Michael Burdener, whose very name connotes a carrier of "burdens." Whereas Burdener's London notebook focuses on his familial insecurities and conflicts with his brother-in-law, Ama's discourse in "A Child of Delicacy" is more probing and energetic – describing, weighing, and re-evaluating. In "The London Notebook" the concealment of the implied author does not mitigate Michael's obsession with himself. Ama is more attentive to her relationships with others. In fact, we learn much more about Michael's ideology from Ama than we do from his own notebooks.

While Burdener's section is written as a kind of revenge confession, the Ama section is written in an almost elegiac tone, a lament for lost love. As she retraces her past – becoming the president's mistress, falling in love with Michael, marrying and having children – she conducts a dialogue with herself. However, Ama can be brutally critical in her dialogues with the voices of the past as she reflects on her "fallen" past as the "dirtywoman" of the redeemer, Kruman – "What could you do with any man," she accusingly asks herself: "Something in you chooses them, Ama Liarcheat" (140–1).

Ama's relationship with Michael is made and marred by ideology. As her teacher, Michael first inspires her with his radical anti-colonial speeches, though he also captures her schoolgirl's love and curiosity: "He was fair game" (128). Michael, as time wears on, takes on different roles in her eyes: "fair game," eccentric instructor who combines biology and ideology, husband, white lover, father of her children, and "anger man."

Ama's section, "A Child of Delicacy," begins in the third person: "Ama sat down for a moment, beside the dusty radio-phonograph, telling herself to take this moment to still all her voices or by the time Mercredi arrived she would be in the same tearful state as last night and no one could save her" (90). Her thoughts are often presented in the form of an imaginative address to her friend from the schoolgirl past, "Mercredi": "I had a dream, Mercredi. Not like the ones you used to solve so simply for me. Different. Like in the moment before your fingers can adjust the microscope into focus" (91). At other times the first- and third-person types of narration are conflated, creating the impression that as Ama recollects her past, she is seeing herself from a distance as another person for whom "her own life then was a strange island of unnatural fear and shame in the sea of pride that had followed Independence." Here she reveals her first encounter with Michael:

"I know how you have been taught," he said. "You have been taught to seek answers. Bloody, foolish, imperialistic mind-warping rot."

The words shocked almost everyone into attention. Who was he so angry at already?

"You must seek questions. You were taught to seek answers because with answers you could be beaten. Stress their inferiority old chap, or you'll get nowhere. And if you run across a bright one, fill him so full of the encyclopaedia he'll not have time to think. That's what the school bosses say to us."

Or something close to that. Heard so many times, in repetition and in inadequacy, how could she now say what were his actual phrases that first time. When her own life then was a strange island of unnatural fear and shame in the sea of pride that had followed Independence.   (128)

The kind of self-consciousness that Ama possesses lends her character a strength and appeal that other characters lack: she admits her *unreliability* and conducts a dialogue with herself, revising her assessments of the past. And as she corrects herself, we come to respect her honesty and trust her characterizations of others. Ama's comments on Michael, for example, could begin to put the reader on a different footing with his character as she presents new evidence.

So far I have dwelt on the differences between the Michael and Ama sections. I want to emphasize that the kinds of sympathy evoked by, for example, the account of Michael's conversations with Gamaliel in "The London Notebook" are even more strongly brought out by the kinds of internal dialogue that are interwoven in Ama's section; that both of them provide us with psychological insights not shown in the other sections; and that they both elicit far more sympathy because of the personal footings they have with the reader: they seem to have the implied author's approval to a more obvious degree than any of the other characters.

The presentation of Michael and Ama tells us much about the ideological biases of the implied author. My own rhetorical reading would note that the strongest disparagements are reserved for the ethnocentric, imperialist characters like the British counseller Firebank or the American CIA agent Rusk; the strongest sympathies are for individuals like Ama. The implied author that I imagine to be scripting this text loads the Michael and Ama sections with much more argumentative appeal than the other sections, and this reflects the implied author's values and politics: the politically non-aligned characters, like Ama, who are more concerned with private existence, are treated more favourably than the conspicuous political agents, the public servants like Geoffrey Firebank or President Kruman.

Godfrey's writing here does show the intersection of personality and social influence. He is not, however, a social relativist. Throughout the novel he loads the dice in favour of certain types of persons and against others. Though he tries to write a novel that is neither just an argument for the autonomy of consciousness nor just an argument for the primacy of cultural determinism, his bias is plain: though he believes that all actions are purposeful, some characters in his novels are assigned more purposive weight than others. While the implied author, in the guise of objective observer, assumes that all human beings can justify their actions, this same implied author doesn't script footings for First Samuels, Rusk, or Kofi Kruman that allow them to attain psychological complexity, to display their reasons for the reader. The implied author cannot conceal his contempt for the men who are the products of institutions and ideology – especially men who are the agents of colonialism, like Firebank, or who are authoritarian, like Kruman. Godfrey's assumption, one that could be objected to, is that such agents of colonialism lead trivial, shallow private lives and that in order to compete in public politics they have lost all emotional sensitivity and sophistication of thought; he suggests that this loss of feeling and introspection is somehow related to their corruption. But how are we to deal with this evaluative screen in the writing?

Irving Howe has written that "one of the supreme challenges" for the novelist is "to make ideas or ideologies come to life." The process results in a transformation of the ideology:

No matter how much the writer intends to celebrate or discredit a political ideology, no matter how didactic or polemical his purpose may be, his novel cannot finally rest on the idea "in itself." To the degree that he is really a novelist, a man seized by the passion to represent and to give order to experience, he must drive the politics of or behind his novel into a complex relation with the kinds of experience that resist reduction to formula – and this once done, supreme difficulty though it is, transforms his ideas astonishingly. His task is always to show the relation between theory and experience, between the ideology that has been preconceived and the tangle of feelings and relationships he is trying to present.   (*Politics and the Novel* 21–2)

Unlike *The Double Hook*, which tends to avoid social and political history by privileging the ideal structures of allegory, and unlike *Beautiful Losers*, which satirizes historiography to promote a dionysian dissolution of the material world, Godfrey's work scripts our reading transaction so that we engage more directly with social and political reality. *The New Ancestors* is an ambitious approach to ideology and individual feeling, a novel that struggles with the kinds of experience that resist reduction to formula. But Godfrey's treatment of character, one might be forced to admit in the end, is not entirely consistent. He transcends the liberal-Marxist disagreement when he depicts Michael and Ama, but perhaps he takes on a more Marxist-oriented approach when ironically depicting Geoffrey Firebank and First Samuels. The reason for this inconsistency is Godfrey's refusal to lapse into cultural relativism. And perhaps this refusal is entirely excusable. Godfrey is sensitive to the distortions that arise from transforming politics into any kind of extended metaphor; yet at the same time he is aware that phenomenological description is not enough, that his experimental novel – unlike, for example, Leonard Cohen's *Beautiful Losers* – must also contain a pragmatically critical, ethical component. I think that our first intuitive response to Godfrey's work would recognize this ethical drive, even in the plot that characters are caught up in: the drama of African nationalism, and the fear of political alienation and reprisals for not supporting the right authority. The most powerful man in Lost Coast, President Kofi Kruman, is portrayed by Godfrey as dangerous and unscrupulous, though his power is displayed in a shadowy, surreptitious underworld – in his stage-managed orgies that celebrate his dominance, in the propaganda mills of his spokesmen, in the swift and deadly tracking down of the young rebels by his army.

Unlike Watson's *Double Hook*, Godfrey's text provides no ideal closure. In the fictional world of *The New Ancestors* he has provided the reader with both the rational political concepts that individuals might formulate and the phenomenological context in which political programs arise. This author is just as interested in the sensuous physical reality in which the characters exist – what they eat, what inspires their appetites, lusts, jealousy, love; what they feel in the hot African weather, the feel of clothing soaked in sweat, the smell of the streets, the shape of a friend's or enemy's facial bones, the internal musing on sights, sounds, smells, and tastes and textures of cloth, wood, metal, water, and skin – Godfrey is just as interested in all of these factors, as they arbitrarily flow into a character's world, as he is in the abstract, rational, political principles and goals in the minds of characters.

In *The New Ancestors* ideology exists in a haze of appetite and feeling. It is true that figures of authority like Kruman are caricatures who are not assigned the special footings that make them appealing to the reader, footings that are scripted for such characters as Michael Burdener and Ama. But one might say that Godfrey is content not to demystify or justify Kruman, nor to explain why First Samuels or Rusk or Burdener becomes an opponent of Krumanism, because he wants readers to wonder about these things themselves. All that the reader can do is trace the impulses to power, the initiations into the rebel attitude, and become, like Godfrey, observers of the public political spaces occupied by these characters and their effects on the private worlds of Michael and Ama.

5 *Badlands*: Remembering and Forgiving the Father's Past

In the Canadian critical parlour the work of Robert Kroetsch occupies a central position. A highly gifted tale-spinner, experimental poet, a collector and fabulator of regional Alberta lore and legend, and a participant in the postmodern writing scene, Kroetsch has held the attention of a wide audience and is described by Linda Hutcheon as "Mr Canadian Postmodern," a writer who "has radically problematized the notions of creativity and commentary" (*Canadian Postmodern* 160). His critical essays, editorial work with the postmodern journal of theory *Boundary 2*, and wide knowledge of modern philosophy and critical theory, as displayed in his own writing and the important series of interviews with Shirley Neuman and Robert Wilson titled *Labyrinths of Voice*, have created contexts that compel readers to look for signs of structuralist and deconstructive activity in his fiction. His novel *Badlands* has been especially interpreted in light of a deconstructive feminist ideology: Connie Harvey has argued that the perspective of Anna in the novel "views male obsessions with adventure, fame and ambition as lunacy, and shows that the men are oppressive and cruel to the women who are not compelled by their vision" ("Tear Glazed Vision" 32). Other critical constructions of the novel have focused on postmodern discontinuity (MacKendrick), the revolutionary force of the female perspective (Seim), or the role of Anna as a trickster who is "learn[ing] how to tell stories" (Lecker, "Freed from Story" 170).

Yet while Kroetsch has obviously been influenced by feminist criticisms of male ways of knowing and being, this rhetorical reader finds much in *Badlands* that does not privilege the feminist perspective of Anna Dawe so much as show her learning about the deadly inertia and solitude of her father's life: Dawe's life ends in unhappiness not just because he is male but because he cannot accept or love men or women. He is unable to create friendships; this is a problem that Anna Dawe also has, but by the close of the novel we can see her over-coming it. I see her as being put through processes of remembering and forgiving, empowering processes that allow her to grow and take action in a way that moves her out of years of solitude and inertia. And there is much subtle sympathy here for the remembrance of male quests as well as for the women who join with and reshape the adven-tures in the *Badlands*.

Neither men nor women in this novel can happily exist in isolation from each other; friendships are what finally bring these characters some measure of fulfilment, even if these friendships involve the imaginative but sympathetic retracing of the steps of a lost parent, as in the case of Anna Dawe and Anna Yellowbird. In fact, the male quest myth – which Kroetsch brilliantly parodies in the figure of Hazard Lepage in his earlier *Studhorse Man* – already contains an im-plicit critique of the hero's wayward wanderings and upholds the joys of reunion and companionship. Kroetsch deliberately sets up an intertextual dialogue with Western male quest fictions, a dialogue that is not only parodic and critical but also celebratory and life-affirming: myths of the returning warrior (Odysseus), of the male hero's journey to the underworld (Orpheus), even of the river voyage (Conrad, Twain) are not simply shown to be futile or useless. The journey is existentially unavoidable; however, the participants in the journey might be a mixed company of supportive men and women, not just men alone.

This is the kind of rhetorical interference I hope to run with the present reading of the novel: the footings that are provided for the women in *Badlands* can be read as scripting some sympathy for the collective energies of the male quest. When the quest is led by the selfish Dawe, however, that collective energy is drained. What we are presented with finally is not simply a feminist deconstruction of the male quest but on urge to reconcile men as a group with solitary men like Dawe, isolated women with forgetful men, daughter with father, child with parent, the present with the past. What this reading em-phasizes is the development of a character's ability to forgive the men of the past and grow, in Anna's case, into an independent agent, able to forge new relationships and move in new directions.

Badlands is mulifaceted: it is *ludic*, critical of Western epistemology and the male will to power over the signified, yet it is at the same time nostalgically enamoured with male quest stories, with the "Western yarn." The Kroetsch that we imagine as the originary consciousness, or the implied author, sets up a seemingly critical perspective on male power in the voice of Anna; but this author also sets up counter-perspectives that neutralize or at least argue against this critical feminist perspective. As we read *Badlands* we can construe voices that are sometimes in disagreement, voices that correct each other, and voices that sometimes correspond and agree that human communities and social bonds are what redeem us.

There are two major addressers in the novel whose rhetoric mediates between the reader and the utterances of all other characters: Anna Dawe, whose comments on her father's field-notes and whose thoughts and self-narration bracket and intrude into the chronologically past narrative of her father's river journey; and, as well, an unidentified addresser who narrates the Dawe expedition story, a voice that is never clearly identified with Anna's consciousness but is, rather, an omniscient voice created by the male Textual Author. Anna Dawe's discourse is on ambiguous terms with male authority and modes of being; the follies of men are sometimes highlighted, but this critique of male being is contradicted by ironic elements that are attached to her own discourse and by the male sympathy that is infused into the expedition section by the style of the implied author. Kroetsch appears to endorse the feminist deconstruction of male authority, yet he still wants to preserve the affirming, fertile, playful aspects of male being.

FEMALE AUTHORITY AND SYMPATHY TO MALE FOLLY

Kroetsch privileges the perspective of Anna Dawe by endowing her voice with a superior intelligence and understanding. Her discourse opens the novel, and she sets up or frames the narrative, explaining and interpreting events for the reader, attempting to guide us to a critical view of William Dawe. Who is Anna Dawe? What does her discourse betray to us regarding her character, her preoccupations, her talents?

I am Anna Dawe. I am named Anna because my father, eleven years after that season of 1916, remembered the Indian girl, Anna Yellowbird, who had, he explained to my mother, saved his life. What he did not explain to my mother was how that Anna – by what violent surgery of the spirit – healed him back onto his feet of clay.

I don't know that I ever received a letter from my absent father. He sent us instead, left us, deposited for me to find, his field notes; God help us we are a people raised not on love letters or lyric poems or even cries of rebellion or ecstasy or pain or regret, but rather old hoards of field notes. Those cryptic notations made by men who held the words themselves in contempt but who needed them nevertheless in order to carry home, or back if not home, the only memories they would ever cherish: the recollections of their male courage and their male solitude.

We read those field notes, mother and I; together we went through those long and slender notebooks, designed to fit a denim pocket rather than a coffee table. We read in those sun-faded and water-wrinkled books, read not only the words but the squashed mosquitoes, the spiders' legs, the stains of thick black coffee, even the blood that smeared the already barely decipherable words. And the message was always so clear that my mother could read, finally, without unpuzzling the blurred letter or the hasty, intense scrawl. She could read her own boredom and possibly her loneliness, if not his outrageous joy.   (2)

The opening paragraphs of the novel set up a male-female, he-us opposition; the male pronoun is the subject acting on the female pronoun as object ("He sent us ... left us"), a relationship that the women will struggle to reverse, to turn themselves from the acted upon into the agents of action, from the isolated, passive, home-bound, reading audience for male exploits to the active travellers, interpreters, notemakers, and players who experience the "joy" of action and contact: the "outrageous joy" of contact with the world of spiders and bloodstains is in fact what will give Anna her later independence.

Anna Dawe's discourse shows her already subverting the role of the passive female audience expected by the male hero: not only is she privy to the secrets of her father that her mother has been shielded from, but she also expresses her knowledge of Anna Yellowbird's saving of her father in the writer's metaphoric, even biblically tinted language: Yellowbird puts her father through a "violent surgery of the spirit," "healed him back onto his feet of clay." Anna's discourse is constructed to show her as knowledgeable about the conjunction of the physical and the metaphysical, mortal "clay" and spiritual surgery. What is striking here, though, is the isolated reading activity of daughter and mother. While they might resent their positions at home, they have not gained Anna Yellowbird's knowledge; they have not been able to obtain this, although neither have they contended that the healing of a father should be their right as well.

The striking metaphoric language of the first paragraph is followed by further evidence of Anna Dawe's knowledge of language, evidence of her intellectual understanding of different genres of discourse: "we are a people raised not on love letters or lyric poems or even cries of rebellion or ecstasy or pain or regret, but rather old hoards of field notes. Those cryptic notations." Anna's syntax exaggerates her careful weighing of her father's actions and her continual modifying and qualifying of her description, an attempt to describe with painful accuracy her father: "He sent us instead, left us, deposited for me to find, his field notes."

Anna's knowledge of different discourses is, however, implicitly compared to the attitude of men "who held the words themselves in contempt," for whom language is a recording of "their male courage and their male solitude" – or, we might add, the pride that pushes them to face their quests alone, to own their victories by themselves, solitary, without the support of others. The men like Dawe believe in the primacy of their own genius, ignorant of the collective effort that enables them to do their work. In fact Anna Dawe is just as isolated as her father and will need to form a strong social relationship with Anna Yellowbird to break out of her inertia.

Anna's opening chapter is presented by Kroetsch as a way of introducing the reader to an intellectually and psychologically astute observer of human affairs: she has worldly knowledge, literary sense, and wit, but she also has emotional insight. Yet Anna's introspection paradoxically sets her both apart from and together with the men who are introduced in the expedition narrative. Anna's thinking about her father is part of a quest for self-knowledge and identity, an excavating of the evidence of the past that parallels the father's search for the bones of dinosaurs; but her search for the past is initially passive, and this passivity is partly encouraged by the legacy she has inherited from her parents that allows her to buy her gin by the case and her books by the parcel. Who *is* Anna Dawe, she persistently asks herself; she explores various ways of placing her identity in some context:

Out of that union, if it might be called such, out of that version of wedlock, I was born into my own silly inquiring.

Why it was left to me to mediate the story I don't know: women are not supposed to have stories. We are supposed to sit at home, Penelopes to their wars and their sex. As my mother did. As I was doing.

And yet I was not Penelope because no man wagered his way towards me. The one who did, ever – the man who violated my inherited dream of myself, if not me – assuming I did not seduce him into it – was gone, not travelling, but into death. And I was alone and I sat in the house inherited from my mother, who inherited it from her mother – a winterized summer place on the shore of Georgian Bay where William Dawe might sit and dimly apprehend across the water, through the coming storms, the west he found and denied; and I was there alone with only my parents' financial acumen to guard me, and I bought my gin by the case, bought and read my books by the parcel, imagined to myself a past, an ancestor, a legend, a vision, a fate.   (3)

Anna is named after the Indian girl Anna Yellowbird and is therefore already collocated with an active principle, but she is also "45, unmarried"; she is a product of William Dawe's "deprivation and repentance and lust" and a product of her mother's need "for an evening's relief from her boredom." In the fourth paragraph, as she spins out her carefully co-ordinated sentences, the reader is again shown an intellectually precise mind, one that deals in endless qualifications and subtle cynicism. Yet she has not yet taken the adventurous flight of the woman for whom she is named.

Anna draws attention to the unconventional – even anti-conventional – power that she has as the "mediator" of the novel, and as an independent woman: "Why it was left to me to mediate the story I don't know: women are not supposed to have stories. We are supposed to sit at home, Penelopes to their wars and their sex." Anna has no lover, "no man wagered his way towards me." She is no Penelope; but neither is she yet an Odysseus. She is rather Homer herself, the storyteller, the mediating consciousness who attempts to hold our attention.

Some critics, pressing for a feminist reading of this section, emphasize Anna's subversion of the Penelope role, or that she refuses the male version of heroic narrative, with the woman as the passive object of male adoration or the passive receiver of male action. Anna is certainly no passive object; yet she is still alone, still inactive, with only her "parent's financial acumen to guard [her]." This supposedly intellectual and literary ability in Anna is not an empowering thing for her; it is partly what debilitates her and connects her to her father's mind-set. The less solitary characters who are not as caught up in the work of the mind do resist the malign influence of Dawe: "Web was the man I imagined most often," she says; "he was the one person whom my father could never destroy; possibly because there was nothing inside him, nothing behind that penis of his, that was destructible" (4). Web's very name suggests that he is connected to life, passion, and people in a more vital way than William Dawe.

Anna's discourse is filled with abstract and paradoxical epigrams: "There are no truths, only correspondences" (45), she says, after comparing herself to the woman in the ranch-house who is isolated, protected, and yet imprisoned in her solitude by her husband. Moreover, Anna's statements about the power of men over women are sometimes subject to ironic contradiction because of her own insights into the men on the expedition.

Anna's interventions continually evaluate and interpret characters for us from a woman's perspective. Yet she also urges us to see her father's field-notes as undergoing a fundamental change because of the Badlands: the change signals isolation, unhappiness, and the loss of spirit. As Anna reads the field-notes, she attempts to identify the point at which her father undergoes the transformation into a man isolated from feeling, love, and camaraderie. In the "mystery of his first season" in the Badlands, she notes the changes in his 1916 field-notes, changes that point to a transformation in the man whose "ventures into deserts and jungles, into Africa and Texas and Patagonia, into the Arctic Islands" she and her mother have followed so closely:

His field notes, after that summer, were less and less concerned with his crew, his dangers, his days of futile prospecting, his moments of discovery, his weariness, his ambitions, his frustrations. They became scientific descriptions of the size and location of bones, of the composition of the matrix, of the methods of extraction and preservation ...

And I had to visit those badlands where his success began. Because, there, in that beautiful and nightmare season – he ceased to dare to love.   (139)

Not all of the men on the Dawe expedition give up their ability to care for others; Grizzly certainly is an important provider of group comforts: as the crew's cook he is particularly important. Even in the section of the expedition narrative where Dawe finally asks Grizzly to find Anna Yellowbird, Anna Dawe pronounces a positive evaluation of his submission to Dawe's arrogant commands: collective charity is promoted by Grizzly's act, and Dawe's isolation is highlighted as peculiar to *his* way of thinking, not that of the whole group: "Grizzly, through the tent flaps, bowed. Perhaps, in that self-effacing gesture, if it was that, he redeemed himself from the depths in the instant he made his entrance ... In his not resisting ... In his letting be, perhaps ... he already knew what Anna was learning, what the others would never learn"(187).

Grizzly's self-effacing "gesture" redeems him from the male selfishness that Anna Dawe has been targeting: these include Dawe's self-aggrandizing quest for the bones that will bear his name and bring him scientific fame and historical immortality; his control over Anna Yellowbird and her love; and his control over his crew. Anna notes the curious sexual control that Dawe attempts to hold over his men as he forbids them to have contact with Anna Yellowbird:

The curious thing about Web is that he obeyed my father's arbitrary command: he stayed away from Anna Yellowbird. And I suppose the curious thing about all those men on our frontiers is the sexual lives they lead. Where

the two most obvious answers to their presumed needs are to love each other
or to share a woman, they will do neither. They avoid violent relations with
each other by violence; the squaw wrestling of their pale bodies is meant to
deny the wrestling of their spirits together. And the notion that a woman is
not to be shared is one of their notions also.

We have the instinct of community, will share or be shared: the avoidance
of Anna was no idea of Anna's. Grizzly, of course, ignored my father's command; he managed to do what he pleased, either because my father thought
of the cook as another woman, or because he was too much the male my
father pretended to be to be put off by my father's bluff.   (162)

"They avoid violent relations with each other by violence," says
Anna Dawe. Male relationships are interpreted as power relationships by this narrator; but these are not relationships that naturally
arise out of the desires of men like Web or Grizzly – Dawe is the one
who is responsible. Dawe is presented as embodying all that is wrong
with an oppressive and overly competitive tyrant: he is not a likeable
team-player. In the expedition story he is presented as always need-
ing to play the patriarch; he converts his crew to *sons*, his progeny, his
products; they exist to supplement his self-pride: "he would have
sons, perhaps he would have three sons, one of them a young man
like Tune, almost morose at times, dreamy, given to singing in the
midst of disaster; young Tune who had learned to worship – yes, that
was hardly too strong a word – Tune worshipping the old master,
Tune already dreaming of his conquests in the field; but Dawe would
be at home, at home with his wife and family"(171).

In the expedition story Dawe continually attempts to assert his authority, sometimes with bathetic effect: he tries to control Web's sex
life; he converts the pathetic bordello pianist Tune into a crew mem-
ber; his greed for the specimens that will bestow upon him scientific
immortality brings all to the brink of collapse and death. He is never
entirely successful, granted, in his attempts to control his crew; but
what is important to note is his constant need to triumph, to win by
stifling the views of others. He is unable to co-operate with others. His
contentious ethos is demonstrated during his meeting with the photographer Sinnott. Sinnott and Dawe are rival experts, but it is Dawe
who attempts to disprove the claims of Sinnott, Dawe who initiates
the competition. Sinnott argues that the past is continually fading,
dying, and can only be captured in its frozen, photographic form; he
claims that he and Dawe are both peddlers of vanished history. But
Dawe assumes that his paleontology is superior, that he actually recovers the past. That there *is* a discernable past is, significantly, the
one thing that Anna Dawe finds her father right about: "on that issue
only, my father perceived correctly" (4).

The presentation of Dawe's meeting with Sinnott emphasizes the former's seeking of superiority in his treatment of history:

Sinnott brushed at his own white beard, adjusted the black patch over his right eye; as if he must now save himself from vanishing. He had already, using Web as his model, adjusted the square bellows camera, set the flap shutter. Taking the rubber bulb in his right hand, he determined that his subject would not only pose but would smile as well. Sinnott announcing: "We are two of a kind, Mr. Dawe, you and I. Birds of a feather. You with your bones that are sometimes only mineral replacements of what the living bones were. Me, rescuing positive prints out of the smell of the darkroom."

"I recover the past," Dawe said. Unsmiling. Adjusting his grip on the sweep. "You reduce it."

"I know," Sinnot said. "And yet we are both peddlers."

"You make the world stand still," Dawe said. "I try to make it live again."

"Then let me save you from your inevitable failure," Sinnott said. "Tell me where you might possibly be reached and I'll send you the consolation of my masterpiece: The Charlatan Being Himself."

Dawe smiled.

Just as the camera clicked they heard the ferryman call out again.   (128)

Dawe's control of his crew elicits hostility, and, converted into resentful sons, the men are drawn into an Oedipal struggle against the father figure who not only controls their labour and their sexuality but also controls the mother-lover figure amongst them – Anna Yellowbird. Dawe's authority converts his crew into a resentful family that seeks escape, or even an overthrowing of the patriarch:

He recognized that the others were watching. Web and Grizzly were watching. They were working, but they were watching too, deciding whether or not to let an impulse make them leave, whether or not to mutiny first, kill him first, or simply to walk out of the canyon, float on out of the canyon and leave the task of killing to the canyon itself, the task of cleaning up after to the hawks, the coyotes:

And he, then, Dawe, slyly, gently, in the way of a loving father, shifted the pencil from right hand to his left; he reached with his empty right hand, gently patted the top and back of Anna Yellowbird's bowed and motionless head.   (224)

The expedition story provides dramatic examples of the negative aspects of Dawe's authority, examples that reinforce the observations of Anna Dawe's inserted commentaries on her father's follies. Anna's intellectual and psychological authority is reinforced by the expedition story, which gives us "proof" that her pronouncements and evaluations of him are valid. But there is a further level at which Anna's persona is associated with a privileged perspective. I have already mentioned that feminist readings of *Badlands* emphasize that Anna subverts the Penelope role (Seim, Harvey). Kroetsch does use mythic subtexts to provide an ironic edge to Anna's commentary. Not only does he use the Penelope-Odysseus story, but he also inserts an incest motif, a version of the Electra story. In the final section of the novel, wherein Anna Dawe meets Anna Yellowbird, she tells the Indian woman how her father came to her as a lover when her mother lay dying – further evidence of Dawe's need to control the roles or identities of the women around him for his own purposes:

And I told her then: that time when he came home from the field; I was fifteen, my mother was dying: he showed up on a blustery day in late October, pretending he had only stepped out to buy a quart of milk, pick up the morning paper, and he could not understand how the door had locked itself behind him: and he came to my room instead of going to my dying mother, his dying wife; and he lay down on the bed beside me; he held me in his arms, held me, and "Anna," he said, "Anna"; and then, in the midst of his maudlin crying he told me; "you were named for that Anna, and she was fifteen, then, too; your mother dying then, too, always dying –"; and he kissed my neck, my shoulders, my young breasts. And I told that Anna. "I was frightened. But I touched his back. And he kissed my breasts –"

And Anna interrupted me. "He was a great one for the nipples." She was standing there in the heat, in the unrelenting sun.   (262)

The Electra element is of course transformed in Kroetsch's text. Anna Dawe, obviously, is not aligned with a "real" father in the way that Electra is with Agamemnon: William Dawe is closer to being the unscrupulous stepfather Aegisthus, whom Electra urges Orestes to murder. Anna directly refers to the possibility of having a brother, or of being born a man herself: "But a son, born of his flesh and blood and blind obsession, might at least have grown up to kill him" (109).

The incest-patricide motif emphasizes the mental bondage to her father that Anna must escape: she must transcend not just the Penelope role, the waiting woman, but also the Electra role, the daughter controlled by her father's fate and alienated from her mother. These are *not* her roles. But the most significant mythic pattern that Kroetsch appropriates for both Anna Dawe and Anna Yellowbird is that of an inverted Orpheus-Eurydice myth. In the traditional male quest for his lost love the male hero is the actor, but the woman is passive. Neither Anna Yellowbird nor Anna Dawe is a

Eurydice figure; nor are they unsuccessful Orpheus figures. Anna's quest for her father's past, and Anna Yellowbird's previous journey (at various points described as a journey to the *underworld*, the realm of the dead), put the women in the *actor's* role: the women search for lost men. What has happened to the mythic parallel? In an interview Kroetsch has said that he is intrigued by a Blackfoot story that reverses the Greek roles of Orpheus and Eurydice: the woman is the active agent:

I have been reading Greek mythology a lot for many years and I researched Blackfoot mythology very extensively ... One that is just spectacular is the descent-to-the-underworld story; I started from the Orpheus figure, naturally, I suppose. But then I read a collection of North American Indian descent stories put together by a Swedish anthropologist. There is an incredible set of connections between the two sets of stories, often most interesting. For instance, in the Orpheus story a man makes the journey into the underworld and is forbidden to look back on his way out. In the Blackfoot story a woman makes the journey into the underworld, and is forbidden to touch her recovered lover on the way out.   (*Labyrinths* 97–8)

In *Badlands* the William Dawe expedition is followed by Anna Yellowbird: "Shit almighty, you don't think she's still *following* us?" says Web to Dawe when Dawe tells him to get that "squaw" to help guide them to the location of the bones. Anna Yellowbird, when she is first discovered by Dawe, appears in a gravesite (6), a shocking "apparition." Later, Anna Dawe says that Yellowbird sought William Dawe because "the hunchbacked man, not the others, ... could find the way to the place of the dead": "At fifteen, newly a widow, having learned that her husband was vanished and gone, with an iron ship bound for something called England, for something called the World War, she had wandered blindly towards the east, knowing that England lay to the east, the war raged to the east; she had listened for the guns, watched for the strange ocean on which an iron ship might float; she wandered disconsolate, desolate, on those western prairies that were taken from her family before her husband too was taken" (148). Anna Dawe's mother, Elizabeth Kilbourne Dawe, actually marries William Dawe because it was *fashionable* to marry the war-bound men: "it was the fashion and rage to marry a man who was going away to die, the deep and secret courtship becoming not only the dreamed courtship of death but the death itself" (191).

This is the Penelope role that both Anna Dawe and Anna Yellowbird need to subvert: they become the empowered women of the Blackfoot myth, companions who have returned from the places of the dead. And Kroetsch apparently portrays them as successful. The final sentences of the novel remind us of the condition set out for the woman who is allowed to recover her dead lover, that she must not turn to look at him as she is leaving the underworld: "We walked out of there hand in hand, arm in arm, holding each other. We walked all the way out. And we did not once look back, not once, ever"(270).

Indeed, "looking back" is the male mistake, the blunder of Orpheus that cost him Eurydice. By using the Blackfoot story or version, Kroetsch reinforces the important power that Anna Dawe and Anna Yellowbird have in sustaining life and breathing life into the past. The women, of course, reconcile themselves to the past by *not* looking back; they recover love, their dignity, and find new friendship – what William Dawe himself should have ended up with on his own quest.

THE VOICE OF THE EXPEDITION

In an interview Kroetsch has said of *Badlands* that he was "playing" with the female narrator, but that there is another level of addresser, the narrator of the expedition story, that is meant to be puzzling:

In *Badlands* I was playing with the woman's first person narration and with the whole notion that a story speaks in what I call the male story. The knight out (the night out!) questing or hunting. The knight, leaving his love in the castle, going out to kill or be killed, and in the process generating desire. A story has its own energy which carries it along and I was letting this happen so that I got a double effect, a playing off between the story and the woman's narration, almost a discomfort for the reader who wonders where the story comes from.   (*Labyrinths* 170)

There is a double narrative in *Badlands* and two different voices. We do wonder why this unnamed narrator and not Anna Dawe tells the expedition story. There are both tensions and similarities between Anna's authority and that of the other narrative perspective. Kroetsch has invested Anna's discourse with authority and wisdom; but this weighty authority contradicts the ideology that she presumably supports because it is precisely like the male ideology that she criticizes. Anna's discourse contradicts itself by professing female values in the male style of omniscience. (Anna assumes that female and male forms of discourse are distinguishable: male authors assume "an omniscience.")

Probably the most important inconsistency in Anna's character, the male folly in herself, is one that Kroetsch seems to have deliberately inserted into her character. Kroetsch has Anna state that her father assumed that she would be free of male folly; but her father's treatment of her actually makes her into his product, a product of a male design; ironically, the father's determinism is to blame for her male qualities. Kroetsch has Anna admit that her father's influence has been profound:

He assumed that I, his daughter, in error not born a son, must by virtue of that error be free of the folly he found in men. And, having made that assumption – in order to assure its validity – he locked me up in the house I had inherited. Or was inheriting ... He locked me up in an education I might as well have inherited, it was so much mine before I realized it was given me; he locked me up in the money I did not know until years later, too late, was not even his to give.

Who could I learn to love, but him? And how, but in his manner? Loving loss as he loved it, finding no live world that was absolute enough to be worth the gaining, he would seek only the absolute of what was gone. His was a heaven of darkness.   (110)

The daughter's inheritance of her father's folly, and her self-critical attitude, begin to play havoc with our perception of this narrator and the argumentative validity of her discourse. If her point of view is meant to be authoritative – and Kroetsch has taken pains to make it so, to provide the complex intellectual, psychological, and mythic dimensions that show her as superior then how can she also be suspect, in error, infected by her father's folly? The implied author has set up the ideological war between men and women as complex and full of paradox: no side is invested with more authority than the other, and the differences between them are often blurred. The authority of Anna Dawe contains equivocations that undermine her arguments against male folly, authority, and ideology. Indeed, if Anna Dawe's criticism is a product of her father's male ideology, then male ideology *is* capable of self-reflection, self-criticism, and improvement. The contradictions in Anna's discourse put her feminist authority under critical pressure and make the binary opposition between the sexes appear simplistic; the implied author is sympathetic to the feminist perspective, but would hope to transcend an either-or conclusion.

An important indicator of the sympathies of the implied author is the tone of the narrator of the expedition section, the "main" story, where most of the drama is contained. There is a discernible disjunction, both stylistic and in point of view, between Anna Dawe's inserted commentaries and the addresser's voice in the expedition sections. This latter narrative voice is anonymous, and although some critics identify it as a product of the imagination of Anna Dawe, it is aligned with a much more authoritative point of view – that of the implied author.

The discourse mask that the implied author assumes in the expedition story is a male discourse mask – or at least one could argue that it is a mask that is sympathetic to male ways of being. The voice of the narrator in the expedition story is tonally different than Anna's. First, the implied author's presentation of male competition is not as harsh and evaluative as Anna Dawe's; the implied author presents the intimate moments in the crew members' lives, those almost pastoral moments of innocence when the men do not compete but simply play:

As the air cooled, Web, to the amusement of the others, suggested they go into the river and bathe: he stripped down, in the evening sunlight, found a bar of soap, leapt into the waist-deep water and waded out to where it was shallower still. He turned his back to the boat and began to scrub at his private parts.

"Don't know if you're getting clean," Tune called, "but the river is getting dirtier."

"Scrubbing up after is half the fun," Web said, rubbing with exaggerated vigour. "Watch me hit one of those geese."

A flock of twenty or so Canada geese, having waddled down from the tall grass on the shore, were daring to swim near the boat; they only abandoned their curiosity when Tune and Grizzly plunged into the water, shivering, shouting. Then, to the surprise of his crew, Dawe himself stripped down naked, for the first time exposing his crippled body: he too leapt into the water.

They swam or bathed or splashed for half an hour, joked, lay on the deck getting warm; and having warmed themselves they returned to the water, again scaring the geese away. Somewhere in the trees an owl hooted and Tune, reminded that he would have to be up at five-thirty, suggested they call it a day. (97)

At other times the men are depicted in quiet scenes of domestic peace – mending, building, or, in the following scene, picking berries and dreaming of the source of the Red Deer River. One could, of course, argue that there is something particularly female about these moments as well. This point could be granted. Still, there is a sympathy extended here to the comfortable intimacy these men share as a group, unworried by competition or Dawe's imperatives; even Dawe sheds his inhibitions in these scenes:

They went into the sprawling patch of buffalo berries and Grizzly spread a tarpaulin under some bushes. Web picked up a stick and used it to beat at the silvery leaves and branches, the small red berries cascading onto the tarpaulin. He found himself enjoying the commotion, the feigned violence, the quiet domesticity – he, beating the bushes, Grizzly scooping the berries together, moving the tarpaulin – and then he was asking Grizzly about that time in the mountains, at the headwaters of the river; and then Grizzly, grunting, picking leaves out of the heaped red berries, was muttering the syllables that might be words like ice, lake, river, forest: and Web, working cheerfully in the hot sun, began to daydream the headwaters of the river, the pristine lakes and the green spruce forest, the trout streams, the glaciers hanging white over the icy waters ... The flies, the mosquitoes, came up at his face, and he went on dreaming the sweetness of the forest, the cool of the glacial calm.   (165)

Here Kroetsch seems to be so attracted to these pastoral moments in male experience that he cannot stop using them to display the affirmative aspects of male being. As well, in such scenes the narrator allows the men greater humour in their dialogue than Anna is allowed in her monologues, providing them with a colloquial, earthy dimension that Anna begins to experience only when she breaks out of her own solitude, abandons the prison of her family house, and becomes friends with Anna Yellowbird.

The implied author in the expedition story takes on the authoritative perspective of the photographer in his style, a way of anticipating the photographs of Sinnott. Each section of the expedition narrative contains a subtitle that reinforces the photographic quality of the scene. The titles (for example, "Looking for the Dead and Missing," 28; "In Which Web Goes Dancing," 77; "Scarlet Lady Sound Asleep," 83) are like the explanatory subject captions for photographs, or like newspaper headlines. As well, the photographic quality is reinforced by the use of sentence fragments and participles that are not accompanied by auxiliary markers of tense and aspect. The captions suggest an attitude of objectivity and accuracy, a disinterested perspective that freezes and analyses actions, a perspective that is quite different from the polemical one of Anna Dawe. The implied author in these sections immobilizes characters in snapshots:

Dawe, watching, deciding.
And the woman also, the girl, watching, staring with luminous eyes at the tall man who bent over her.   (6)

In the first section where this voice appears the reader is presented with a series of "close-ups" of Web and his environment; by focusing on details, the narrator provides us with the real fragments of perception that the characters themselves must disentangle and interpret in the bonefields of the Badlands:

Web combed his fingers through the abundant grass, carefully picked the berries. When his left hand was full he raised up his head, he let himself rest, his haunches on his heels, the ferocious red of the heaped berries held almost to his darting tongue. He glanced around before eating: and only then did he notice about him in the growth of new poplars, not just the one low roof he remembered vaguely having bumped, but the scattering of roofs. They were set a few inches off the ground, on stout pegs, each narrow unpainted roof six to eight feet in length, one of them partially shingled, each constructed of boards that were weathered grey now. Web stood up: and there in the green light of June, the odour of balsam sweet and sticky on the air, he might have come to a buried village, only the roofs left visible to the hot, climactic sun.   (5)

The narrator's voice in these sections displays a phenomenological empathy with the perceptions of the men while also presenting an objective, cameralike eye on the story of the expedition. It provides us with sympathetic insights into male ways of being that are at odds with Anna Dawe's views.

The equally strong presentation of the implied author's male sympathy and Anna Dawe's critique of her father reflects Kroetsch's ideological ambivalence: he wants to hold both positions, even if they are mutually exclusive. Kroetsch does create a real intratextual correspondence between the two voices of narration, a correspondence that sets up an arena in which the reader may see that male and female discourses are not opposed but often in accord. Both discourses long for the vision of collective happiness and strength.

At the end of the novel Anna's point of view and the male sympathy contained in the expedition sections are actually conjoined; she speaks of her father now more with pity and sadness than with anger: "The pathos of their winning through. So brave and so stubborn and so proud, those men. And yet how sad, to think they had risked their days, their lives, everything for that little ceremony of success" (256). Anna recognizes that her father's mistake was his self-imposed confinement after he completed his expedition, his failure to connect with family and friends after his success: "he had kept making field notes for the twenty years after his last trip into field. While he laboured and hid in the museum, when he might have been remembering, or regretting or explaining, or planning, or dreaming or hating, or even loving I suppose, he was busy putting down each day's tedium and trivia. Shutting out instead of letting in. Concealing" (269).

Anna Dawe does not repeat her father's mistake: she throws his notes into the lake and walks away, a friend with Anna Yellowbird. Freed from the position of being the passive reader or audience for her father's exploits, she (and Kroetsch) releases the reader and herself for the writing of a future that includes people like Anna Yellowbird and not just the solitary world of her father. As she walks away, not looking back, I as a reader feel the satisfactory sense of narrative development that comes from imagining Anna Dawe's personal evolution and believing – even though this belief is an effect scripted by the form of the text – that her rhetoric will now no longer depend on the confining voice and experiences of her father.

6 *Burning Water*:
Serious Motives for Play

In George Bowering's major fiction – *Burning Water* (1980), *Caprice* (1987), and *Harry's Fragments* (1990) – the conventions of specific genres, subgenres, and discourses are cited, alluded to, ironically echoed, and parodied. Whether revising the historical biography of George Vancouver in *Burning Water*, or reconstructing a Canadian version of the American Western novel with a female poet and tracker called Caprice, or experimenting with the form of the spy novel in *Harry's Fragments*, Bowering is unmistakably a highly playful and intertextually sophisticated creator of postmodern works. Yet there are deeper political and ethical components in his writing as well, even though he is reluctant to be explicit on these matters: his writings can be read as often giving voice to those groups that have traditionally been marginalized or disempowered in the popular literary forms – women, ethnic minorities, and natives in the Western in *Caprice*, for example – and often imply that the violence, competition, ethnocentrism, and misogyny inherent in popular forms can be challenged and subverted through comedy. Bowering's rhetorical strategies in these novels create personal, equal, and solidary footings with the imagined audience: the voice of narration in his works is gently ironic, modest, droll, casual – seldom does it use a footing of impersonal authority or condescending superiority. The narrative personae in these works are friendly and urbane.

In *Caprice* the traditional Western's thrust towards melodramatic conflict is used, but it is supplemented with a slower-paced comedy of ironic observation; in this Canadian Western, good meals, friendly baseball games, and small-town decency are contrasted with the competitive and murderous habits of sociopathic American gunslingers. This concern for difference and the viewpoints of others is used both seriously and parodically in the opening of *Caprice*:

If you had ordinary English eyes, you would have seen late-morning sunlight flooding the light brown of the wide grassy valley and making giant knife shadows where the ridges slid down the hillsides, free of trees, wrinkles made in a wide land that didnt seem to be in that much of a hurry ...

But if you had those famous Indian eyes you could look down into the wide valley and see something moving, maybe a lot of things moving, but especially one black or at least dark horse, which meant probably a rider too, and in a little while a rider for certain. (2)

In *Caprice* and in *Burning Water* the narrator consciously tries to show that the European gaze does not see perfectly, that it is selective and interested and myopic – it doesn't yet see the approach of horse and rider. One might object that Bowering is substituting one cultural stereotype for another by referring to the sharpness of the Indian eyesight; however, in the larger context of these works, this criticism would be a highly simplistic reduction of the multiple levels of irony that Bowering is working with. There is a subtle political side to these novels, even though the ludic side is so prominent. In *Caprice* Bowering refers to the different views of a scene that can be experienced, depending on whether you have "normal reader's eyes" or those of a "curious reader" (34). The following reading of *Burning Water* is not as playful as the author might have wished for, for it is done with the rhetorical lenses of a "serious" reader.

A political and ethical edge can be read in the themes and rhetorical structures of *Burning Water*. Here Bowering parodies the historical version of the quest, the history of the explorer, the scholarly accounts of George Vancouver's life and voyages. This is a work that resembles Kroetsch's *Badlands* in its reluctance to be overtly ideological, to promote an identifiable politics yet also present a revised history. The novel is ambivalent concerning social authority; but although it ostensibly eschews notions of social determinism, in practice it makes significant use of psychological analysis and ethical judgment.

Burning Water certainly contains marks of postmodern playfulness, aleatoric plotting, and self-reflexivity: this metafictional history combines description of George Vancouver's charting of the Pacific coast with humorous speculation on the private lives and conversations of the crew, with fanciful depictions of the ironic attitude that the west-coast Indians might have had to the peculiarities and obsessions of the white explorers, and with a self-reflexive story that shows how Bowering, during sabbaticals in Italy and Central America, made a series of accidental "discoveries" that relate his experiences to those of the explorer Vancouver. The happy accidents and coincidences in Bowering's own exploration of the Vancouver story are an important part of his method and authorial attitude. In fact, the pre-positioned author shows that he is open to random experiences, an honest historiographer, one without predetermined methods, plans, or values: he hopes to be free from ideological constraints.

But though in *Burning Water* Bowering uses techniques that emphasize his anti-determinist and ludic attitude to language, he also inserts causal psychological explanations when describing Vancouver. As well, he focuses on specific types of power conflicts: he has mounted a critique of male modes of competition, militarism, and pride that reflects an ideologically interested position, not an ideologically innocent one.

FIRST-PERSON INTRUSION AND THIRD-PERSON DRAMATIZATION

There are various addresser-addressee levels in *Burning Water*. Bowering's distrust of "transparent" fiction is shown by his attention to his own acts of narration: the implied author steps forth in the prologue in the form of an "I" narrator who introduces the reader to his fictional procedures in a casual, affable tone. The "I" narrator is avoided in the rest of the novel, but still repeatedly enters in an "I" narrator's voice. The implied author attempts to move away from the "I-you" addresser-addressee relationship by referring to himself or dramatizing himself in the third person: he reduces himself to the level of his characters, a "he," while drafting his readers into an intimate company of "we." The levels of addresser-addressee relations include an "I" narrator who is explicitly identified as the implied author, a "he" character who is also the author, and a series of other discourses assigned to characters like Vancouver, Quadra, and Menzies that are mediated by the implied author / narrator:

When I was a boy I was the only person I knew who was named George, but I did have the same first name as the king. That made me feel as if current history and self were bound together, from the beginning.

When I came to live in Vancouver, I thought of Vancouver, and so now geography involved my name too, George Vancouver. He might have felt such romance, sailing for a king named George the Third. What could I do but write a book filled with history and myself, about these people and this place?

... So I began to plan a novel about us, about the strange fancy that history is given and the strange fact that history is taken. Without a storyteller, George Vancouver is just another dead sailor.

How could I begin to tell such a story? I asked myself. Books do have beginnings, but how arbitrary they can be. Get away from Vancouver, I said, and went back to Trieste, as far eastward as you can go in western Europe, among seafaring Europeans or their descendants, to do it for real this time, their story ...

A block from my hotel was a Roman theatre, across the street from the police station. Men in togas, at least in the summer sunshine, used to stand in the square and feel the sun on their foreheads.

And that same sun shone upon the thousand miles of coast they were all getting ready to fight for ...

So we Georges all felt the same sun, yes. We all live in the same world's sea. We cannot tell a story that leaves us outside, and when I say we, I include you. But in order to include you, I feel that I cannot spend these pages saying I to a second person. Therefore let us say *he* and stand together looking at them. We are making a story, after all, as we always have been, standing and speaking together to make up a history, a real historical fiction.   ("Prologue")

In the prologue the narrator is presented as an innocent observer of history, one who has not consciously pursued the story of Vancouver's expedition but has seemingly had the subject brought before him through a series of chance coincidences: name, place, and literary profession have happily mixed to provide him with the opportunity to write of George Vancouver. This discourse puts the narrator on a personal, informal, yet authoritative footing with the reader. In the first three paragraphs the narrator sets up a distinct temporal progression while simultaneously preserving the random and illogical connections between his identity and the figures around him named George. The syntax of the first two sentences, with their opening subordination, signals the author's careful arrangement and weighing of ideas. Bowering does not move through a discernible hierarchy of stages but through a series of playful circularities: the suspense of "When I was a boy" is followed by the ordinariness of "I was the only person I knew who was named George"; the "but" raises our expectations for some interesting antithesis, but we are merely given an exception to Bowering's boyhood discovery: "I did have the same first name as the King." The "When ... but" sentence structure is followed by other paragraph openers that offer the syntactic suspense of an argument ("When ... so", or "In the ... so") but instead lead us into circular reflection.

These nominal resemblances and circular musings suggest that "current history and self" are bound together. The narrator certainly reinforces the postmodernist's subjective attitude to the past: the observer's or interpreter's goals and values colour one's evaluation of the past. Reassuring reminders of identity are found through nominal evidence. The lack of finer discrimination and analysis here serves to impress upon the reader the implied author's artlessness and naïveté. In fact, the "When I was a boy" opening sets up a functional tenor of discourse of boyish innocence that is maintained in the remainder of the prologue.

The implied author's strategy is designed, thus, to emphasize the author's ingenuousness; but the prologue is also an opportunity to promote his historiography: "the strange fancy that history is given and the strange fact that history is taken." Bowering's "fancy," what he imagines happens, is that historical understanding, a conscious relationship to the past, simply falls into the lap of the "chosen" by fortune; he trusts chance and random inspiration. But he also contends that history is a fiction, a social construct that is "made up" by writers: "Without a storyteller, George Vancouver is just another dead sailor." Emphasizing random play and social construction, the narrator is faithful to postmodern anti-realist principles. But he is also faithful to something that is not quite postmodernism: a belief in a universal humanism. He attempts to promote a form of social unity by linking all men to some common denominator; individual differences of time and place paradoxically become unimportant in Bowering's subjective world because they are united by similar phenomenological experiences: "So we Georges all felt the same sun, yes. We all live in the same world's sea. We cannot tell a story that leaves us outside, and when I say we, I include you."

In his prologue the narrator undermines conventional authorial power through a self-effacing attitude, through acknowledging his subjectivity, through asserting that history is either a random and haphazard collection of facts (whose interpretation is more of a matter of serendipity than logic) or a biased selection of personally interesting conclusions and connections from the detritus of history. He builds assent in the reader as well by having us feel we are participants in this fiction, participants who stand beside him looking at the creation of this historical fiction: he promises to reveal his own history-making process by putting himself into the story as a third-person "he."

The narrator's other first-person intrusions into the story display a distrust of authorial omniscience and objectivity. His own twentieth-century postmodern position is opposed to the discussion of "abstract values." He displays his own postmodern transcendence of eighteenth-century intellectual obsessions in a barely restrained sarcasm:

[William Blake] was operating in that small city called London at the end of the eighteenth century. Everybody knew everybody, and yet when they produced satires they took great pains to make sure you readers did not read the real names but you knew who was getting it. And they spent a lot of time, it seems to me, commenting about abstract values they all professed to sharing and accused one another of mishandling. I mean taste, virtue, honesty, modesty, piety, that sort of thing.   (24)

First-person address often leads the narrator here to reiterate his original promise that he would set up his authorial functions not transparently but explicitly; when he comments on the thoughts of Vancouver, he foregrounds his use of the omniscient mode and comically announces that as a novelist he has the privilege of omniscience. Such a reminder serves to draw attention to the fictionality of the novel and demystifies the narrator's authority. This type of intrusion reinforces Bowering's commitment to an exposed or foregrounded writing process:

[George Vancouver] never wrote down on his charts any names that were there before he got there. He didn't imagine that one should.
 "And certainly (for novelists have the privilege of knowing everything) he thought a great deal about" readers far in the future, as far as London and Lisbon, about what they would read when they uncovered his charts. They would read the depth of water, the true configuration of the shoreline, and the name that pressed through his exact head at the exact time that he was required to set ink to surface.   (63)

First-person intrusions, however, do not always serve to expose the implied author's act of narrating; these intrusions also reinforce the authority of his interpretation of Vancouver. The narrator has already admitted his subjectivity; but such an admittance is rhetorically calculated to win our approval of his honesty and lack of art – this is the rhetorical figure of *paralepsis*, professing to deny that which the author is doing in the act of speaking. He uses rhetorical strategies in the process of declaring his rhetorical innocence. The narrator does set himself up as an authoritative commentator on the life of George Vancouver, a perspective that is meant to give us true insight into the cause of his quarrel with Menzies, the ship's surgeon and botanist. The narrator presents himself as possessing casually those truths of Western society that Vancouver was just beginning to realize:

Commander Vancouver wished he could have been winning Nootka back from the French or the Russians, instead of taking it back by agreement from the Spanish. At least the French and the Russians he had no trouble disliking. Still, had that been the case, Don Juan would at this moment be home in San Blas.

War may make men go around the world, but love makes the world go around. Actually, any novelist, any man of imagination could have told him that commerce was the moving power behind both. (75)

The narrator or implied author as a first-person intruder must carefully insert his interpretation of the causes of the Vancouver-Menzies conflict because he risks breaking the illusion of disinterestedness, the guise of not knowing the truth. In a send-up of a heavily subordinated, left-branching eighteenth-century sentence, the implied author seems to catch himself in the act of being an asserter of the truth, then twists away:

If the truth be known, and of course we are in a position to know it, or whatever purchase one makes on the truth in a work of imagination, if that is what we are engaged in, that being the entire issue we test here, Vancouver did not really have anything against Dr. Menzies. He was really angry at Banks, not his agent. He hated Menzies, that is true, but it was the hatred for an obvious token, not the anger he reserved for the adminstrator of the Royal Society. Better a botanist than an agent of the fur trade, for instance. (84)

But despite the implied author's attempts to wriggle free from the position of epistemological authority, he cannot help but insert evaluative and interpretive commentary on Vancouver, even if it is in the guise of mediating the thoughts of another character. In fact, when he relays the thoughts of Archibald Menzies, the ironic perspective on both Vancouver's pride and Menzies' rationalism is apparent:

Archibald Menzies slept in his customary bedclothes, the covers in his hand held to the side of his head, the candle lit beside his last-minute book of physic. He was satisfied to accumulate knowledge. He was an eighteenth-century man.

Not for him the necessity and the pride of that youth [Vancouver] who was *ne plus ultra* and must now be also *rara avis*. (50)

How do the kinds of discourse tactics employed by Bowering in the first-person narrative mode compare with those he uses in the dramatized third-person mode? In the first-person mode the implied author seems interested in three effects: first, to persuade the reader that he is artless, casual, and is discovering his "story" through accident; second, that although he has no ideological bias, he is above the abstractions and rational values of the eighteenth-century mind, that he has transcended *their* hypocrisy; third, to draw attention to or foreground the fiction-making process in order to convince the reader further that his method is "honest" and authentic, not a transparent "window" but an open activity in which artifice is exposed. This theoretical self-reflexivity is designed to let readers know that they will not be entranced by any "illusions" of epistemological authority and objectivity.

These effects of the first-person intrusions are reinforced by the use of the third-person dramatization of Bowering's authorial activities. When we read of his sojourn in Trieste, we understand that he is again using the tactic of self-deflation; the fog of the Adriatic that blurs his vision sets up a comparison of himself to the dreamy poet-Indian in the opening scene who imagines ("fancies") that the European ships are giant birds or even the vessels of gods, and who is chastised by an older Indian fisherman: "That is your fancy speaking. That can be very dangerous for people such as us. You must never believe that you have seen a god when you have seen a man on a large boat" (17). Bowering would compare himself to the confused young Indian who is having his vision altered by the more experienced Indian.

The implied author's dramatization of himself as a character *does* draw attention to the artificiality of fiction as well. He does foreground the fiction-making process; he depicts himself struggling with the writing of this self-reflexive historical fiction and remembering that pure realism is much easier: "All the confusion made him think about the good old days, when the realist novelist just had to describe the setting and introduce into it the main characters. He could have told you a hundred things he had seen in Trieste. For instance the guy with no legs in the rain on the Corso Italia"(23).

Third-person dramatization not only functions to persuade the reader that the implied author is artless and to foreground the fictionality of the novel; it also sets up the author in a journey that parallels the sea journey of Vancouver: the author places himself on the same level of character as Vancouver, then looks for the significant connections between his experiences and Vancouver's. The third-person dramatization shows the implied author trying to find personal analogues that might allow him to imagine better what life aboard Vancouver's ship was like. Bowering, in a playful and comic gesture, juxtaposes Vancouver's resentment of Menzies with an authorial musing on the size of the ship's deck and its relation to the distance between bases on a baseball field:

I [Vancouver] cannot set anchor but the little porridge-eater is off in one of my boats, having commandeered two of my men, to dig up another obnoxious weed, to make a home for it upon *my* planks, and to sequester yet more canvas to make it a roof from the rain, as if it had never felt the rain in this desert!

The vessel is ninety-nine feet long, and he hopes to cover all of it, I'm certain.

[shift to authorial self-dramatization] Trying to keep that straight in his mind, he imagined the distance from home plate to first base, add two steps. Or say from the red-checkered line to the end boards, to be more patriotic, i.e. loyal to the power brokers in the east. (33)

As Bowering dramatizes the authorial persona, he shows himself in his travels coming upon small and pleasing accidental parallels with Vancouver's travels: while writing in his notebook, he discovers the stamped outline of a sailboat on its cover (80), the Chinese manufacturer's trademark; while wandering in a Tuscan palace, he discovers a sixteenth-century map-room with the names of sea-coasts that Vancouver was trying to locate or remap (35–6); while eating sauerkraut in a trattoria (coincidentally the anti-scurvy dietary requirement that Vancouver was infamous for using), he muses on the amount of time that a traveller spends in planning his meals (66); while riding his bicycle back from the credit union in Vancouver, he notes that he is travelling on Puget Drive, named after one of Vancouver's officers, Peter Puget (149); while in a Costa Rican museum the author discovers an eighteenth-century *bicorno*, the hat worn by Vancouver (192). In Venice he depicts himself riding the *vaporetto* alone to the Lido to look at the Adriatic (55); in Trieste, without news or mail from his family, friends, and home in Vancouver, he feels the explorer's sense of isolation (62); and while in Central America he comments: "If he could just bring Captain Vancouver to being as alone as he had made himself" (217).

Why does the implied author wander haphazardly around the globe, purporting to be exploring Vancouver's life? He gives us a partial answer:

He had gone east to Trieste because the Europeans had come west and now he was going south to Guatemala because they had come north. They had come north in the summer, and he was going south in the winter. He did not know, to be sure, why all this, but he trusted it, though as the voyage grew longer and the books got thicker he felt himself resting more and more on his faith in the readers: would they carry him, keep him afloat? He thought so. The B-747, filled to capacity with people and baggages, touched the earth like a giant bird touching down on the sea.   (173)

The author whom we imagine to be controlling the text expresses a "faith in the readers"; this is another way of scripting an equal footing with the reader, a footing employed at the outset when he attempted to persuade us that "we" were aligned with the author and not simply the receivers of a one-way monologue. Now he surrenders control over narrative coherence and logic to the reader's interpretive abilities.

But the narrator's dramatization of his accidental finding of connections to Vancouver in far-away places is rather more than an illustration of the uses of serendipity. He stumbles upon preserved artefacts, fossil traces, vestiges, echoes, and resemblances from Vancouver's time and his surveying of the Pacific. What do these connections mean? Bowering's accidental discovery of connections seems, on the one hand, to embody a metaphysical belief that "history is given" (as he remarks in the prologue): "When he found those things he knew a book was going well, that is without oars, before a good wind. Or he could be forgiven for thinking so. At times like that one did not necessarily believe in magic or its practitioners, the gods; but at times such as those one knew it was happening to itself rather than waiting around for him to think of it"(145). On the other hand, even while history is disclosing itself to him, Bowering is not simply relaying this information in a transparent form, but has selected, edited, and provided ideological filters for the reception of his story. He has also acknowledged in the prologue that history is "taken."

THE CRITIQUE OF MALE AGONISM

The function of the narrator's first-person interventions and his dramatization of himself in the third person is partly to persuade the reader that the implied author is ideologically innocent; his openness and honesty are supposedly markers of this disinterested position. The travel notes attempt to show that historical understanding can be "found" through serendipity, that indeed new discoveries or breakthroughs in knowledge can sometimes be arrived at through accidents. But Bowering deliberately sets up the story of Vancouver as a tragedy of the male will-to-power, a critique of rational men fighting for dominance. The implied author attempts to win our faith in his self-awareness by being playful and ideologically innocent; yet his presentation of power and authority shows assumptions about values, and implies beliefs in causal psychological interpretations of character – and this is wholly to be expected, for even an adherence to a ludic position carries with it implicit ethical or serious imperatives. The power preoccupations of Bowering underlie his professed disinterestedness and neutrality: Bowering is fascinated by Vancouver's quarrel with Menzies, and he is interested in criticizing Vancouver's use of power.

The narrator does much to "naturalize" the implied author's activity and persona, to present himself as a vigorous, happy, and free individual, unburdened by tragedy or neuroses. But in contrast to this self-portrait, the implied author turns Vancouver into a deformity, a neurotic "other" who will stop at nothing to achieve fame. The narrator makes it clear that he believes that male competitive drives are behind Vancouver's expedition. In his psychological assessment of Vancouver, Bowering emphasizes the commander's hunger for fame, his need to live up to the example of his father figure, James Cook (45), and his quest for historical immortality: "He wanted to be a famous story very much, the kind of story that is known before you read it. He wanted his name and exploits to be a part of the world any Englishman would walk through"(62). The implied author constantly intrudes to emphasize the competitive, agonistic aspects of Vancouver's character; and these intrusions are subtly laced with authorial judgment, an implied criticism of the boyhood playing at war that Vancouver has not outgrown.

Vancouver's attraction to Quadra is everywhere framed as suspicious and unnatural, and the implied author notes how it leads to discontent amongst the crew. The contradiction of a Protestant Puritan Englishman's love for a Catholic who indulges in lavish banquets and displays of finery is shown as a source of rancour for the English crews: "the members of the British crews were still grumbling about their commander. For while he was tremendously cordial with the Spaniards of all conditions, he was strict, cold, aloof, and businesslike with his own offices and men"(194).

The implied author's judgment of the follies of male competition are perhaps most strongly dramatized in the ironic treatment of the Vancouver-Menzies conflict. Vancouver's quarrels with his botanist are partly rooted in the previous conflicts of his mentor, James Cook, with scientists (34). And Vancouver has even more reason to hate

Menzies because of the threat to his authority that the Scotsman represents. As the ship's surgeon he violates Vancouver's sense of control, for he could "make an estimation of the events transpiring inside" the individual: "He could scan the face and read the vitals, augury that no client can forgive" (73). The implied author is careful to emphasize the competitive nature of Vancouver's relations with Menzies, for Vancouver sees in Menzies all the talents that he considers he possesses himself – "intelligent, curious, thorough, disciplined, professional" – mixed with his own pride, "the kind of pride that would not allow him to say 'Yes sir' when he was thinking 'No, sir'" (95). The implied author speaks with an irrefutable wisdom when he describes the foundation of their hostility to each other:

Of course the source of the coolness between the two men was complex, but it involved the definition of work and worthwhile activity aboard a military vessel. Vancouver, as was to be expected, wanted to be in the Atlantic or the Carribbean, sinking French ships; yet here in the North Pacific he proved his officers and crew the best explorers, navigators and map makers in the world.

Menzies, for his part, was more interested in extending the limits of human knowledge about life than he was in ending it; so he was not averse to cutting into a body to explore and map that shore, even if once in a while he had to end the life of a flying or crawling exemplar. (178)

According to the implied author, there is a causal psychological explanation for the conflict between Menzies and Vancouver, a conflict that is so important to the narrator's rhetorical purposes that he constructs a fictional murder climax, with Menzies getting revenge for the destruction of his plant specimens by killing Vancouver with his pistol. (In fact Vancouver ended his life under rather less spectacular circumstances in Surrey, England.) By making the murder of Vancouver into the conclusion, the implied author moves from ludic post-realism into direct criticism: this implied author sees Vancouver as a tragic example of the male will-to-power, the male competitive mode. The implied author has actually set up the life of Vancouver as a morality play while professing to being objective, to being an innocent witness to history.

One of the recognized scholarly accounts of Vancouver's career, Bern Anderson's *Life and Voyages of Capt. George Vancouver: Surveyor of the Sea* (1960), is a source of some of Bowering's excerpts from letters, observations on ship's discipline, diet, and crew psychology, the description of Menzies' shooting of an albatross, and numerous other facts. There are obvious ways in which *Burning Water* and this conventional history of Vancouver differ. Anderson's account of the parting of Vancouver and Menzies is much less dramatic than Bowering's: "Vancouver's relations with Menzies were seriously strained at times, but they were cleared up without the need for formal action" (223). Bowering's *Burning Water* seems to attempt to address those aspects of Vancouver's life that Anderson's history could not dare to accommodate, and in an evaluative, iconoclastic tone that the objective historian by definition could not use: the drama of male competition, the absurdity of their ethnocentrism, sexual jealousy, and power struggles are all presented by Bowering. Anderson offers a physiological explanation for Vancouver's lack of good relations with his men: his "chronic hyperthyroid condition," resulting in "irritability, bursts of energy, unexpected loss of temper, and fatigue" (67); but Bowering as a novelist can dramatize Vancouver's feelings and actions, and need not cover the strange habits of men at sea in the euphemisms of objective description.

Unlike the objective style of Anderson's history, Bowering's postmodern style, registered in the prologue and in the self-reflexive narrators and authorial self-dramatization, supports the demystification of historical discourse, the revealing of the storyteller's tricks. However, underlying Bowering's "Heracliteanism" and serendipitous approach to history is his deliberate focus on certain types of male competition and power conflicts. Bowering's interest in exposing power conflicts, by targeting the male will-to-power, is teleological, argumentative, and didactic; this is an interest that fits uncomfortably with the postmodern aesthetics of ludism, but it is an interest that is unavoidable.

A rhetorical intervention into the site of *Burning Water* shows how shot through with power this work is, how it mobilizes a serious critique while posing as ingenuous play. The postmodern rhetoric of liberation and open-endedness here does involve the inscription of new authority and new belief.

7 *The Handmaid's Tale*: Dystopia and the Paradoxes of Power

Margaret Atwood has consistently written about women who are both powerful and vulnerable, strong enough to endure and retain a sense of self yet unable to elude the grimmer aspects of entrapment. Often Atwood's protagonists are writers or artists themselves and therefore have particular creative resources to help or even hinder them – Joan Delacourt in *Lady Oracle* (1976) is a writer of costume Gothics; Rennie Wilford in *Bodily Harm* (1981) is a lifestyle journalist; Elaine Risley in *Cat's Eye* (1988) is a painter. What will be considered here in greater detail is the voice of the most obviously entrapped artist-writer in Atwood's novels: Offred in *The Handmaid's Tale*.

This novel has received a great deal of critical and popular attention since it was published in 1985. Perhaps the popularity of *The Handmaid's Tale*, adapted into a film directed by Volker Schlondorff in 1989, can be attributed partly to the convenient opportunities it provides for teachers in the Canadian critical parlour to explain its generic inheritance from dystopian fiction (Orwell, Kafka, Zamyatin, Huxley) and to the postmodern design of the novel. Critics have been especially attracted to its metafictional elements and narrative frame. Among eight articles on *The Handmaid's Tale* published since 1987, four give prominence to the effect of the "Historical Notes" section on our reading. Out of these four, Amin Malak, Arnold Davidson, and Harriet Bergmann emphasize that the "Historical Notes" are an ironic treatment of the failure of male academic readings of the oral record left by Offred; the future historians fail to treat Offred's experience with compassion or emotional sympathy. As Davidson suggests, the

Notes section is perhaps the most depressing part of the novel since it shows how little has been changed by Offred's discourse: the male oppression of women has persisted in a different form beyond the post-Gilead period, even into the aboriginal Republic of Denay. W.F. Garrett-Petts goes further and argues that the Notes section actually marginalizes and reduces the character of Offred to a mere shadow: he tries to show that her character is significantly deflated by the time we reach the end of the Notes. Constance Rooke, by contrast, asserts that Offred's character retains integrity and cannot be divorced from the politics of resistance.

Other tasks undertaken by various critics include the explanation of generic sources (Malak, Lacombe), the identification of motifs of nature and womanhood (Rooke, Rubenstein, Friebert), and the attempt to infer that Offred's metaphorically significant real name is "June" (Rooke, Rubenstein, Friebert).

Very little of the above criticism deals with the voice, ethos, or style of the narrator in *The Handmaid's Tale*. Only Lucy Friebert comments that the voice of Offred is the same "low-keyed" one that "B.W. Powe derides as 'virtually interchangeable' in all the previous novels." Friebert defends this monotonous voice by arguing that this "voice, approximating the limited scope of Offred's life symbolized by the blinkers on her veil, is precisely what makes *The Handmaid's Tale* credible" ("Control and Creativity" 286).

Amin Malak says that although Atwood is writing in an Orwellian tradition, the novel "sustains an ironic texture" and is not filled with as many "frightening images" as Orwell's *Nineteen Eighty-four*: "the few graphic horror scenes are crisply and snappily presented, sparing us a blood-curdling impact. Some may criticize this restraint as undermining the novel's integrity and emotional validity" ("*The Handmaid's Tale* and the Dystopian" 14). I agree that Atwood's narrator does not present as many overtly "frightening images"; nevertheless, the narrator does consistently evoke a violent atmosphere that accords with the evil totalitarian regime. In fact Atwood's narrator is a powerful user of language, a poet and rhetorician who presents in a strategic way the true horrors perpetrated by the Gileadan state. Although in the "Historical Notes" we learn that the overall narrative arrangement is not Offred's, that her taped oral utterances have been transcribed and arranged by Pieixoto and Wade, the power of her rhetorical stance is distinctive and unusual.

Harriet Bergmann has recently written that "Offred was not, we can tell, a person who cared particularly about the written word before the establishment of Gilead" ("Teaching Them To Read" 850). Actually, we don't know many details about the reading and writing habits of Offred before Gilead: we do know that she was university educated, that she loved books, and that she worked transferring books to computer disks. We should keep in mind that we are meant to read Offred's story as one composed retrospectively – and an extraordinary retrospective it is. Offred demonstrates immense skill in constructing her rhetoric; this "unskilled" storyteller pays expert attention to narrative point of view, to physical detail, and to remembered conversations. Indeed, Offred's discourse reflects a practised devotion to *written* rhetoric. And of course, one of the great compositional problems of the novel is that the *oral* qualities of Offred's taped discourse are always *imaginary* oral qualities: as we read the printed discourse, we attend to a complex syntactical and rhetorical play that is the product of the economy of writing, not speech. What we need now is an analysis of the paradoxical ways in which the language of the narrator scripts special footings of intimacy and authority with the reader.

In *The Handmaid's Tale* Atwood is caught in the dilemma faced by many creators of satiric dystopias: the author needs both to condemn particular social injustices and to portray the mechanisms of oppression as credible enough, as sufficiently powerful and seductive, to represent a believable evil, not an irrelevant or far-fetched one. While attempting to balance ethical interests with plausibility, the ambitious author risks falling into either transparent didacticism or a contradictory fascination with the rhetorical machinery of dystopic horror. Atwood's discourse is marked by stylistic and rhetorical features – habits of syntactic and lexical arrangement and strategies of managing point of view and addresser-addressee relations – that show she has succumbed to the latter: scenes of violence and horror meant to illuminate sites of oppression are also strategically designed to manipulate and horrify. Atwood's narrator is an authoritative and authoritarian storyteller, one who manipulates the reader as she tells her story but one who is also caught in the web of Gileadan power politics. Offred's powerful narrative skill conflicts with the powerlessness, the innocence, and the descriptive phenomenological cast of mind that also characterize her. It is as if Atwood's skill as storyteller continually intrudes, possessing her narrative creation. Narrative self-consciousness, in fact, does explicitly and strategically emerge.

To see *The Handmaid's Tale* as ideologically and rhetorically problematic is not a "politically correct" view, at least if one considers the majority of the above critical opinions, which aim at solidifying the conventionality of the text by inscribing it in an already readable canonical genre (dystopia, political satire, postmodern subversion), by deciphering allusions, or by weighing the effects of framing devices like the concluding "Historical Notes" section. Only Frank Davey and Chinmoy Banerjee have recognized how the novel "participates not only in various literary conventions and bourgeois assumptions about the self but in various commercial formulas for capitalist book production" (Davey, *Reading* 84) or how "Atwood is concerned with the aesthetic enjoyment of a particular kind of victimization, and not with a critical examination of its determinant relations" (Banerjee, "Alice in Disneyland" 80). Atwood's politics in her earlier fiction have been cogently analysed by Larry Macdonald as being fraught with contradiction (as are also, Macdonald points out, the fictions of MacLennan and Davies) because of the reduction of collective problems to "the psychic wounds of individual characters" and the tendency to undercut the possibilities of positive political change: "these novelists end by urging individual adaptation to a status quo which their fiction simultaneously urges upon us as intolerable" ("Psychologism and Progress" 122).

The Handmaid's Tale is similarly caught in contradictory discursive impulses: it shows a world that is "intolerable," but it cannot avoid complicity in using the mechanisms or rhetoric of that very intolerable world. Hence, a trope that might characterize the rhetorical gestalt of the novel is *paralepsis*, the figure of verbal dissimulation and duplicity that asserts its lack of rhetoric while using rhetoric, that on the one hand critiques authority and on the other is complicitous with that authority, that feigns powerlessness in order to wield power, that disavows deliberate arrangement while arranging words with great care: "I'm sorry there is so much pain in this story," Offred apologizes, then proceeds to make us wince with her sharp, "fragments, like a body caught in crossfire or pulled apart by force" (279). By examining these and other instances of such discursive contradictions and paradoxes, I will provide a close reading of the novel and subject key sections to lexical, syntactic, and rhetorical analysis; I will try to get a grip on the authority and style of Atwood's storyteller while remaining close to the play of addresser-addressee relations, those social relations that metonymically reflect the implied storyteller's attitude to power.

THE AUTHORITATIVE VOICE OF THE VICTIM

In *The Handmaid's Tale* the reader is addressed by a narrator whose authority is sanctioned by the implied author: she possesses an analytical intelligence that demonstrates her clear superiority over others. She is a reader of the social "signs" in her environment and in everyday objects. Offred is assigned the authority of an implied author; there is, in fact, no gap between implied author and narrator, no attempt to distinguish the voices. There is, however, a tension between Offred's narrative skill and the characterization of her as a Handmaid. This narrator wants the discourse freedoms and powers normally granted only to men; yet she is in the position of Handmaid:

The pen between my fingers is sensuous, alive almost, I can feel its power, the power of the words it contains. Pen is envy, Aunt Lydia would say, quoting another Centre motto, warning us way from such objects. And they were right, it is envy. Just holding it is envy. I envy the Commander his pen. It's one more thing I would like to steal.   (196)

The intelligence and wit of the narrator is but one of various rhetorical tactics that Atwood uses to induce our acceptance of the didactic authenticity of her satire. Its social and intellectual validity as argument is enforced by a narrator who shifts between readerly footings of intimacy and equality to footings of authority, superior insight, and impersonal detachment. In the opening first chapter of the novel we are guided through the world of Gilead by a narrator who surveys her surroundings with a highly developed analytic sense, who possesses a writerly skill in evoking shapes, odours, and images:

We slept in what had once been the gymnasium. The floor was of varnished wood, with stripes and circles painted on it, for the games that were formerly played there; the hoops for the basketball nets were still in place, though the nets were gone. A balcony ran around the room, for the spectators, and I thought I could smell, faintly like an afterimage, the pungent scent of sweat, shot through with the sweet taint of chewing gum and perfume from the watching girls, felt-skirted as I knew from pictures, later in mini-skirts, then pants, then in one earring, spiky green-streaked hair. Dances would have been held there; the music lingered, a palimpsest of unheard sound, style upon style, an undercurrent of drums, a forlorn wail, garlands made of tissue-paper flowers, cardboard devils, a revolving ball of mirrors, powdering the dancers with a snow of light.

There was old sex in the room and loneliness, and expectation, of something without a shape or name ...

We yearned for the future. How did we learn it, that talent for insatiability? It was in the air; and it was still in the air, an afterthought, as we tried to sleep, in the army cots that had been set up in rows, with spaces between so we could not talk. We had flannelette sheets, like children's, and army-issue blankets, old ones that still said u.s. We folded our clothes neatly and laid them on the stools at the ends of the beds. The lights were turned down but not out.

Aunt Sara and Aunt Elizabeth patrolled; they had electric cattle prods slung
on thongs from their leather belts.   (13–14)

The first chapter contains an odd mixture of clarity and obscurity,
hard detail and shadowy impressionism. The plural subject of the
first sentence – "We" – and the institutional gymnasium setting signal
a makeshift group cohesion, the unity of refugees, the homeless, prisoners, or recruits in some military training camp. By the end of the
third paragraph we understand that they are somehow all three. The
second paragraph, drawing on a particular cultural stereotype mark-
ing women as the receivers of male sexual agency, hints that they are
women; when they are named at the close of the chapter, we know
their sex.

The narrator's language indicates that she has detached herself
emotionally from any memories associated with the gymnasium.
(The past tense, "slept," indicates that this is a memory.) The language that she uses to describe the gymnasium in the second sentence
is unusual because it is a more elaborate or expanded description of
the commonplace than we are used to: she isolates in separate "snapshots" features of the floor – the "varnished wood," the "stripes and
circles," the "hoops for the basketball nets" – in the language of a person who is culturally distant from the place and the events that the
gym was designed to host.

The emotional detachment in the tone of the narrator, an emotional
emptiness, matches her surroundings: the gym, a place formerly
meant for players, activity, and spectators, is empty; the hoops are
stripped of their nets (netting has a delicate, membrane-like sensual
quality, a quality absent from the gym). The rather long third and
fourth sentences that complete this first paragraph sustain a ghostlike
atmosphere in which human activity has ceased and all that remains
are inanimate forms like the balcony, which "ran around the room,"
and vague odours that set off memories of tastes, images, and sounds
in the narrator's mind. However, we are not expected to read the
tastes, images, and sounds in these sentences as mere mental projec-
tions: the narrator's tactic is to present these as if they are present in
the very room, ghostly presences that can be excavated by a consciousness sensitive enough to do so. The faint smell is "like an afterimage," hovering in the gym air, and the adjective clause "as I knew
from pictures" is subtly inserted after the image of the "watching
girls, felt-skirted" in order not to disturb the immediate impact of it
as a raw perception of a tangible presence. Of course, this presence is
but a shadow of the original; its faded and intangible quality, however, is what Atwood's narrator could be trying to get us to appre-

hend. In the third sentence the narrator remembers the former fashions and changes in dating styles that the gym once was host to – basketball games give way to high-school romance; men and women playing competitively turn into different types of players. In the fourth sentence the sense that the gym is literally *haunted* by the past is even more forcefully conveyed: the past-perfect verb cluster ("would have been held"), which suggests an already expired action, is followed in the second clause by an ongoing sound: "the music lingered, a palimpsest of unheard sound, style upon style, an undercurrent of drums."

As Atwood's narrator asyndetically tacks on modifying adjectival phrases, the language suggests both increasing action and increasing danger: the neutral "style upon style" shifts to the menacing "undercurrent of drums," then the surprising "forlorn wail," and finally the tragicomic carnival atmosphere of the death-dance suggested by the "flowers," "cardboard devils," "mirrors," and shadowy dancers powdered with "a snow of light."

Throughout this excerpt from the brief first chapter Atwood attempts to present the narrator as an innocent, a mere observer, a describer of her surroundings; this is a procedure that is retained in subsequent chapters. Chapter 2 begins "A chair, a table, a lamp" (17). (The opening of chapter 2 and other meditations on physical objects and perception uncannily echo sections of Zamyatin's *We*, the obvious prototype for *The Handmaid's Tale*: "Are you familiar with this strange condition? You wake at night, open your eyes to blackness, and suddenly you feel you've lost your way – and quickly, quickly you grope around you, seeking something familiar, solid – a wall, a lamp, a chair" 148).

Offred just happens to "notice" things. But her innocent eye always manages to present us with ideologically significant comparisons, observations, and details; this may hardly be surprising if one grants that ideology is partly an extension of material circumstances. But there is an incompatibility between Offred's narration and the position of subjugation she occupies as a Handmaid. One might wonder why and how such a narrative intelligence could be subjugated in this way. Of course one could argue that Atwood is suggesting that if Offred can be enslaved, anyone can be. Atwood needs to convince us that this Handmaid was subjugated, that the oppression she experienced was evil: the rhetorical intelligence of the narrator is meant to emphasize the power of the regime and the changes wrought upon society. When we finally read the Historical Notes, we also learn that the tale is meant to be read as an experience remembered, as a story recollected in a rather different setting from that of Gilead. However, even before we acquire this contextualizing information, we apprehend that the first chapter contains the polish of arrangement and aesthetic management of a narrative originating from a position of literary sophistication.

What I am trying to suggest is that Atwood's narrator in this novel does not speak entirely in the voice of the victim, the writer who pleads "Mayday"; rather, she speaks in the skilled voice of the rhetorician and the fabulator who is purposefully telling a story. Atwood has the narrator move through her thoughts in a plain style, joining modifying phrases to the main clause on the right side of the sentence, as if to suggest syntactically the artlessness of the narrator. (See Cluett, "Surface Structures," for a detailed analysis of paratactic and right-branching syntax in *Surfacing*.) The co-ordinate structures and right-branching sentences, however, are filled with an abstract lexis, a lexis of contemplativeness that emphasizes the narrator's wisdom, her philosophical and emotional superiority over those around her: "We yearned for the future. How did we learn it, that talent for insatiability? It was in the air; and it was still in the air, an afterthought, as we tried to sleep, in the army cots that had been set up in rows, with spaces between so we could not talk" (14). (The rhetorical question here is another indicator of the author's artfulness.) Here we encounter a paradox: the voluble narrator speaks confidently and precisely about the silence she endured. To increase the sense of the macabre sinisterness of the setting, Atwood's narrator plays on the tension between the domestic softness and military harshness, between the cozy flannelette sheets and "Aunts" and the rough "army-issue" blankets and menacing "electric cattle prods slung on thongs" (14).

ORCHESTRATIONS OF HORROR

The implied author's sanctioning of the narrator Offred suggests that the social world – its architecture, commodities, semiology – is open to systematic rational analysis: historical and political meanings are embedded everywhere; ideology is ubiquitously inscribed. Yet Offred is depicted as fascinated with the paradoxes of power. Offred's ethical assumptions would suggest that she is opposed to irrational modes of argument and persuasion; she is opposed to the tyranny of propaganda. Yet this ethical consciousness demonstrates its attraction to the rhetorical efficacy of violence, power, and the grotesque: Offred has, in her discursive practice, started to play the game of power politics like a true Gileadan.

Time after time Atwood's narrator demonstrates her ability to seize upon seemingly banal objects – a braided rug (17), the walls of a room (61), a pat of butter (108), a chair (120) – and turn them into receptacles or symbols that have resonant metaphysical and political implications. Partly this is meant to illustrate the state of mind of an individual living in an ascetic and puritanically monotonous world: she is hungry for sensuous experience. Not only does this tactic supplement our sense of the repression and boredom in the Handmaid's life, but it also leads to an epiphanic moment – one of those moments that expose how Offred always knows much more than she says, that she possesses powers of apprehension that are impressive. Atwood has endowed this narrator with conspicuous gems of compressed wisdom:

I sit in the chair and think about the word *chair*. It can also mean the leader of a meeting. It can also mean a mode of execution. It is the first syllable in *charity*. It is the French word for flesh. None of these facts has any connection with the others.

These are the kinds of litanies I use, to compose myself.

In front of me is a tray, and on the tray with three slices of brown toast on it, a small dish containing honey, and another plate with an egg-cup on it, the kind that looks like a woman's torso, in a skirt. Under the skirt is the second egg, being kept warm. The egg-cup is white china with a blue stripe.

The first egg is white. I move the egg-cup a little, so it's now in the watery sunlight that comes through the window and falls, brightening, waning, brightening again, on the tray ...

The sun goes and the egg fades.

I pick the egg out of the cup and finger it for a moment. It's warm. Women used to carry such eggs between their breasts, to incubate them. That would have felt good.

The minimalist life. Pleasure is an egg. Blessings that can be counted, on the fingers of one hand. But possibly this is how I am expected to react. If I have an egg, what more can I want? ... I slice the top off the egg with the spoon, and eat the contents.   (120–1)

In the phenomenal world around her Atwood's narrator can find objects that remind her of her condition, that are models of the female life. It is important to note that the "litany" of chairs and eggs is in the "Birth Day" section, a chapter that presents the special birth ritual attended by the Handmaids: the pregnant Handmaid, Janine, literally gives birth – lays her egg – while seated in a special "birthing stool," a chair that allows the Commander's wife to sit behind and above the surrogate mother. The meaning of the word "chair" and the reflection on eggs takes on special significance in this context and contradicts the narrator's disclaimer that "none of these facts has any connection with the others," her need to retain an appearance of being artless, natural, spontaneous. The kinds of meanings that the narrator seizes on are connected to power and mortality – general concepts, to be sure, but concepts that are specifically linked to the exercise of power and the reminders of mortality that are dramatized when Janine gives birth (135–6). The birthing stool in retrospect is ambiguous. The mother can achieve prominence and power; or, if she fails to deliver a healthy child, a sentence of death.

The connection of birth to death, the fine line between power and failure, fertility and sterility, reflects the tendency of the narrator's mind to explore the ambiguities in her world, to delve under the affirmative and pull out the darker intimations of death. She utilizes this procedure when contemplating the egg: the two eggs, one on top of the other, are like a model of the Gileadean birth scene, with the Commander's wife seated up and behind the Handmaid. Offred begins with the neutral description "the egg is white"; she then moves into a figurative language that is resonant with female symbolism: the egg is compared to the moon; the moon becomes a desert; the desert, a place of spiritual trial and of revelation. An alternating emphasis between fertility and sterility, energy and entropy, is played out – the egg literally seems to throb with temperature changes: "The sun goes and the egg fades. I pick the egg out of the cup and finger it for a moment. It's warm. Women used to carry such eggs between their breasts, to incubate them" (120).

In this section the narrator's opening disclaimer would have us believe that her litany is artless, a stream of unconnected facts. Syntactically Atwood's narrator would have us perceive her thoughts as spontaneously stitched together: there are few logical connectors – however, moreover, therefore – that indicate argument. But there is a propositional cohesion here in the very juxtaposition of birth and death images. As I have already noted, one of the justifications for having the narrator produce these longish meditations – and displaying heightened sensitivity to the ordinary – is to portray the severe hunger for stimulation: Offred says, "In reduced circumstances the desire to live attaches itself to strange objects" (120). At the same time, these meditations give us insight into the narrator's cast of mind: her values, fears, preoccupations. And what is highly significant in these preoccupations is that existing beside the analysis of the social condition of women is an attraction to pure power: "I slice the top off the egg with the spoon, and eat the contents" becomes an aggressive movement, a power signal.

There are times when Offred's discourses (or litanies, as she calls them) become redundant, a static piling up of grotesque descriptions. Unlike the previous examples, wherein the meditation upon the object yields a surprising turn, a transformation of meaning, a revelation of similarities, the presentation of the hanged men in chapter 6 involves the continuous reiteration of horror:

We stop, together as if on signal, and stand and look at the bodies. It doesn't matter if we look. We're supposed to look: this is what they are there for, hanging on the Wall. Sometimes they'll be there for days, until there's a new batch, so as many people as possible will have the chance to see them.

What they are hanging from is hooks. The hooks have been set into the brickwork of the Wall, for this purpose. Not all of them are occupied. The hooks look like appliances for the armless. Or steel question marks, upside-down and sideways.

It's the bags over the heads that are the worst, worse than the faces themselves would be. It makes the men look like dolls on which faces have not yet been painted; like scarecrows, which in a way is what they are, since they are meant to scare. Or as if their heads are sacks, stuffed with some undifferentiated material, like flour or dough. It's the obvious heaviness of the heads, their vacancy, the way gravity pulls them down and there's no life any more to hold them up. The heads are zeros.

Though if you look and look, as we are doing, you can see the outlines of the features under the white cloth, like grey shadows. The heads are the heads of snowmen, with the coal eyes and the carrot noses fallen out. The heads are melting.

But on one bag there's blood, which has seeped through the white cloth, where the mouth must have been. It makes another mouth, a small red one, like the mouths painted with thick brushes by kindergarten children. A child's idea of a smile. This smile of blood is what fixes the attention, finally. These are not snowmen after all.

The men wear white coats, like those worn by doctors or scientists ... Each has a placard hung around his neck to show why he has been executed: a drawing of a human foetus. They were doctors, then, in the time before, when such things were legal ...

What we are supposed to feel towards these bodies is hatred and scorn. This isn't what I feel. These bodies hanging on the Wall are time travellers, anachronisms. They've come here from the past.

What I feel towards them is blankness. What I feel is that I must not feel. What I feel is partly relief, because none of these men is Luke. Luke wasn't a doctor. Isn't.   (42–3)

The description of the executed men hanging on the wall exemplifies Atwood's narrator's penchant for the horrific. Presented as an innocent or guileless observer of her world, Offred in fact is an effective tale-teller; but while seeking to condemn the violence around her, her protracted gaze implicates herself, for she has made the vision and instruments of horror into objects of voyeurism rather than symptoms that point to more complex power problems.

This section is a skilfully orchestrated set-piece that begins tentatively and builds to higher levels of shock. Each paragraph takes us gradually and teasingly closer to the horror. Offred begins with a general declaration of the purpose of this display, "so as many people as possible will have the chance to see them." With the deft editorial camera eye of a Hitchcock, Offred avoids a direct description of the bodies and instead focuses on the unoccupied hooks set into the Wall. The pacing in this second paragraph is methodical and slow: sentences are cohesively joined with lexical repetition – anadiplosis and anaphora – as the narrator gradually moves from a plain description of the hooks, "set into the brickwork of the Wall," then shifts to shocking comparisons that carry an indirect hint of amputation and bodily injury: "The hooks look like appliances for the armless." And the final figurative comparison in this paragraph literally denotes the suspended questioning, the deliberately suspended interrogation: "Or steel question marks, upside-down and sideways."

The third paragraph serves up images that are more calculatedly grotesque: first the faceless "dolls," then the "scarecrows," and finally the "sacks, stuffed with undifferentiated material." Atwood's narrator skilfully intensifies the implied danger by keeping the face of violence just out of sight. It is the tension between the *absence* of life and the dead *weight* of the body that is effectively captured here; Offred's language is ponderous and weighty, but spiritless.

The fourth paragraph continues Offred's carefully paced revelation of the object of danger. The narrator begins to focus our gaze ever more closely on the covered faces of the hanged men, "the outlines of the features under the white cloth, like grey shadows." The metaphors in the last two sentences here reflect a typical tactic of Offred's for evoking the grotesque: an innocent, childhood image, a "snowman," metamorphoses into something more sinister, more tragic. The climax of this progression is finally reached in the fifth paragraph: "But on one bag there's blood, which has seeped through the white cloth, where the mouth must have been." But Offred continues to exploit the shock of the tension between childhood innocence and the bloody evidence of the execution. The blood on the face of the victim is "a child's idea of a smile. This smile of blood is what fixes the attention, finally. These are not snowmen after all."

After this detailed description, how do we read and react to the narrator's comment after she tells us that these victims were doctors who had performed abortions in the years before the present regime?

"What I feel towards them is blankness. What I feel is that I must not feel. What I feel is partly relief, because none of these men is Luke. Luke wasn't a doctor. Isn't"(43). The narrator asserts her "blankness," perhaps an emotionally protective measure to help her cope with the loss of Luke. But the presentation of her perceptions reveals much about her attitude to the reader and the scene she has witnessed: that she must orchestrate the feelings evoked by the scene in a deliberately shocking way, a rhetorically powerful way; that the impact of horror is as important as the reasons for it (and, after all, the Gilead authorities *are* setting the men up as human "scarecrows"); that a reader must experience the event's emotional impact before she or he can be introduced to its political or social background (i.e., the treatment of doctors as war criminals).

One might object that Offred is not meant to be seen as a character who is controlling the reader's perceptions, that the horror in her presentation is simply meant to illustrate how the authorities of Gilead have mastered the art of frightening its people: Offred is simply testifying to the effectiveness of the rhetoric of the Gileadan police state. However, the type of discourse that Offred uses does not simply inform us that the executed prisoners are frightful deterrents: Offred carefully constructs a narrative that makes the reader look at the objects of horror in a prescribed and suspenseful way, a way designed to increase the shock effect. Again, the evidence suggests to me that Offred is intensely aware of the power structures around her, that she is not naïve. When she compares the "one red smile" on the hanged man's mask to the "red of the tulips in Serena Joy's garden" (43), she advances a disclaimer that we can barely accept as valid: the obvious pun that relates the red mouth to the "tulips" is irresistible. As a reader, I am compelled to read the narrator as the originary force behind the pun, that she is well aware of the connections, but that she is simply witholding her comments:

I look at the one red smile. The red of the smile is the same as the red of the tulips in Serena Joy's garden, towards the base of the flowers where they are beginning to heal. The red is the same but there is no connection. The tulips are not tulips of blood, the red smiles are not flowers, neither thing makes a comment on the other. The tulip is no reason for disbelief in the hanged man, or vice versa. Each thing is valid and really there. It is through a field of such valid objects that I must pick my way, every day and in every way. I put a lot of effort into making such distinctions. I need to make them. I need to be very clear, in my own mind.   (43)

"I put a lot of effort into making such distinctions," Offred says. But what distinctions are they? She gives us a glimpse of the philosophical and analytical interest in her mind, then abruptly stops. This seems to be an instance of Atwood's standing too close to her narrator, then shifting to limit the character's knowledge so that it does not merge with that of the omniscient author.

I have been trying to argue that Atwood's narrator is a deliberate storyteller, one who manipulates the reader as she tells her story, and that this shows how she has become caught in the web of Gileadan power politics. This sense of narrative skill conflicts with the power-lessness, the innocence, and the descriptive phenomenological cast of mind that characterize Offred. It is as if Atwood's skill as a storyteller keeps possessing her creation. The storyteller's self-conscious power, in fact, emerges at the end of chapter 7, a chapter that begins with a night-time series of fantasies of the past. Offred remembers her friend Moira, her mother, and her daughter:

I would like to believe this is a story I'm telling. I need to believe it. I must believe it. Those who can believe that such stories are only stories have a better chance.

If it's a story I'm telling, then I have control over the ending. Then there will be an ending, to the story, and real life will come after it. I can pick up where I left off.

It isn't a story I'm telling.

It's also a story I'm telling, in my head, as I go along.

Tell, rather than write, because I have nothing to write with and writing is in any case forbidden. But if it's a story, even in my head, I must be telling it to someone. You don't tell a story only to yourself. There's always someone else.

Even when there is no one.

A story is like a letter. *Dear You*, I'll say. Just *you*, without a name. Attaching a name attaches *you* to the world of fact, which is riskier, more hazardous: who knows what the chances are out there, of survival, yours? I will say *you*, *you*, like an old love song. *You* can mean more than one.

You can mean thousands.

I'm not in any immediate danger, I'll say to you.

I'll pretend you can hear me.

But it's no good, because I know you can't.   (49–50)

There is no hint of this narrative self-consciousness in the opening chapter of *The Handmaid's Tale*, no indication that the story is meant *to be read as if originally spoken*; only in the "Historical Notes" do we learn that the text is meant to be a transcript of a tape recording. But as well, there is no explicit signal in the introduction, such as the title-page to Richardson's *Pamela* ("In a Series of Familiar Letters from A Beautiful Young Damsel to Her Parents"), or the preface to

Nabokov's *Lolita* ("The Confessions of a White Widowed Male"). Atwood's withholding of the contextualizing information creates a gap between our initial, heuristic reading of the book, a reading in which the narrator's authority is valorized through its writerly surface structure, and our retrospective reimaginings and rereadings that are informed by the "Historical Notes" (i.e., our retrospective reimaginings or our rereadings that postulate an oral consciousness rather than one originally cast in *writing*).

Offred's direct address to the reader emphasizes the artificial order that fiction imposes on reality: recognition of this artificiality is supposed to be consoling because "then I have control over the ending. Then there will be an ending, to the story, and real life will come after it." Yet Atwood's narrator wants her discourse to be *more* authentic than fiction, to have a privileged validity as a record of the *real*: "It isn't a story I'm telling." But if Offred's discourse is meant to be "like a letter," with a written sense of addressee, then why have the addressee markers been excluded from the earlier parts of the novel, especially in the introductory chapter?

I contend that Atwood's text compels us to see her narrator in two ways that are not entirely congruent: as innocent recorder and as a skilled self-conscious rhetorician and storyteller. Atwood needs to delay the revelation of this latter rhetorical self-consciousness because a self-dramatized narrator is immediately suspect, immediately prone to charges of unreliability and cunning artifice. And even when Atwood dramatizes the narrator in a self-conscious mood, as in the above, she inserts disclaimers, hoping to retain a sense of Offred's essential artlessness: the tale is a story she's telling "as I go along." Later, in the "Salvaging" section of the novel, Atwood has her narrator again profess that her discourse is artless and innocent: "I'm sorry there is so much pain in this story. I'm sorry it's in fragments, like a body caught in crossfire or pulled apart by force. But there is nothing I can do to change it" (279). These apologies function to convey the ingenuousness of the narrator; but the stylistic evidence that we have gathered so far – her use of symbolic cultural objects, her deconstructions of them, her ingenious comparisons of images that connote power and mortality, her skilful rhetoric, which guides the reader to a special state of suspense and horror – these aspects of the narrator's discourse contradict her professions of artlessness.

The "Historical Notes" provide a significant shift in discourse. This is a peculiarly more comic section than the preceding narrative by Offred, and by being so is subject to ironic criticism. Ostensibly, these notes provide a gloss on the social, historical, and political origins of Gileadan society, as seen by a future society of scholars. The notes provide certain details that are not made explicit in the narrative (the escape of Offred to Canada, via Maine; the reasons for the extreme measures in the birthing process – disease, pollution, war, the President's Day Massacre). But more importantly, these "Historical Notes" are a further reinforcing of the *authority* of Offred's narrative: the academics are satirized as trivializers of history. They have turned Gilead into a matter of textual authentication and an occasion for levity and entertainment. The scholars are pompous cultural relativists; as Professor Piexoto defends his objectivity, Atwood sets him up as hopelessly insensitive to Offred's story:

Allow me to say that in my opinion we must be cautious about passing moral judgments upon the Gileadeans. Surely we have learned by now that such judgments are of necessity culture-specific. Also, Gileadean society was under a good deal of pressure, demographic and otherwise, and was subject to factors from which we ourselves are happily more free. Our job is not to censure but to understand. (*Applause*)   (314–15)

Piexoto's attempts to "establish an identity for the narrator" (315) are meant to be seen as demonstrative of his insensitivity to the text. Offred's story has not been understood by these scholars, who are rather poor readers of texts.

Since Offred's narrative is superior to that of the "Historical Notes," we should remind ourselves of how it operates, what kinds of discourses it contains, and whether these discourses are adequate to the task of exploring the power relations that she has targeted for criticism. I have tried to show how Atwood privileges the voice of her narrator in a paradoxical manner. The implied author attempts to suggest that Offred is ingenuous and artless. But she is unable to do this consistently because the intelligence and aesthetic knowledge of the writer, the storyteller, continually break through. Offred presents evil as both seductive and repulsive, an attitude that could be described as deriving from romanticism and the Gothic (see Banerjee, "Alice in Disneyland" 83–4; Mandel, *Another Time* 138–9). Frank Davey, in *Margaret Atwood: A Feminist Poetics,* however, argues that "the Gothic element is a red herring" because it represents the distorted perspectives of Atwood's protagonists (specifically in *Lady Oracle*) who "lie and fantasize," "fictionalize on derivative models," and "exaggerate goodness and villainy, exaggerate the similarities between goodness and villainy" in order to escape from reality (65). We can remind ourselves, thus, that Gothic involves an element of parody and that an ironic poet like Byron or an ironic novelist like Jane Austen in *Northanger Abbey* deliberately undermines Gothic elements while using them. However, Davey also notes that there is a tension in Atwood's work between the objects of criticism and her own style, between the "rational, analytic, and male" mode of being and the "aphoristic, 'worldless,' and gestural" female mode: "Male order may constitute a travesty of female chaos and its gestural language, but only a wary appropriation of that order enables a speaking of either" (55–6).

Satire is a form that cannot effectively manifest itself through "gestural" and cryptic language: the object of satire must be perspicuously framed (see Banerjee). However, in *The Handmaid's Tale* there is a peculiarly ambiguous attitude to male modes of power and authority. Atwood's narrator is made to observe much that is politically repugnant, but her discourse contains a powerful rhetoric that derives from the ethos of Gilead: Offred is preoccupied with power and authority. What kinds of lexical collocations with power and authority are found in Offred's language? She tends to emphasize tactics and techniques: one of the most significant collocates of power is "vision," or the dynamics of observation – the power of the observing subject and the observed object.

CONTROLLING THE OBSERVER

In *The Handmaid's Tale* the motifs of *vision* are an important part of the presentation of the politics of sexual control: these motifs connect masters to slaves, Commanders to Handmaids. The desires of both are controlled by state regulations: sex has been reduced to reproductive duty without contact and love; Commanders are forbidden to have contact with Handmaids in private. In Gilead even mere visual contact is severely regulated – Handmaids must not be looked at by men, nor may they look at men themselves. When Offred sees the Commander lurking near her room, she describes the act as a form of violation like "the signals animals give to one another: lowered blue eyelids, ears laid back, raised hackles. A flash of bare teeth, what in hell does he think he's doing?" (59). Handmaids in Gilead have their vision obscured by the white winglike hats they must wear in public, making it "hard to look up, hard to get the full view, of the sky, of anything. But one can do it, a little at a time, a quick move of the head, up and down, to the side and back. We have learned to see the world in gasps" (40). This presentation of the regulation of vision expresses the subjugation of the Handmaids (and their patient subversion, "in gasps"). No one is permitted to look at others freely, especially with desire; the exceptions are those agents of the state, Atwood's version of the thought police, the Eyes, who cruise the streets in the black vans "with the winged eye in white on the side. The windows of the vans are dark-tinted, and the men in the front seats wear dark glasses: a double obscurity" (31).

In these visual motifs the power structure consists of the observer and a vulnerable object of vision. But this power structure is prone to reversal: the weakness of being observed is translated into the power of the controlling observer when Offred deliberately manipulates the Guardians:

As we walk away I know they're watching, these two men who aren't yet permitted to touch women. They touch with their eyes instead and I move my hips a little, feeling the full red skirt sway around me. It's like thumbing your nose from behind a fence or teasing a dog with a bone held out of reach, and I'm ashamed of myself for doing it, because none of this is the fault of these men, they're too young.

Then I find I'm not ashamed after all. I enjoy the power; power of a dog bone, passive but there. I hope they get hard at the sight of us and have to rub themselves against the painted barriers, surreptitiously. They will suffer, later, at night, in their regimented beds. They have no outlets now except themselves, and that's a sacrilege.   (32)

This use of the vision motif emphasizes the ambiguities of the power structure in Gilead and carries the implied author's belief that no matter how rigidly controlled master-slave or agent-object relations are, there will always be a point at which the observer is changed by that which he is trying to observe and control. Atwood thus questions the validity of the simple master-slave dichotomy: who really possesses power? The lover or the object of love? The desiring agent or the desired object? Can these agent-object relations be transcended?

Atwood presents Offred not simply as the object of subjugation but as possessing power herself: the power of the powerless, of the seductive prey. Atwood is continually tempted to endow Offred with the strength appropriate to a heroine, but instead she assigns the spectacular heroism to Moira, who mounts a daring escape from the Red Centre, an act of such dizzying audacity that it frightens Offred and the others, who "were losing the taste for freedom" (143). Offred is not a Moira: when she is tempted to steal something from Serena Joy's living-room, or a "knife, from the kitchen," she admits that "I'm not ready for that" (108). Offred, however, is assigned the kind of consciousness that both appropriates and transcends the power politics of Gilead. The implied author seems to privilege the female existential will, the realm of private consciousness, as an adequate recompense for her enslavement: "My name isn't Offred. I have another name, which nobody uses now because it's forbidden ... I keep the knowledge of this name like something hidden, some treasure I'll come back to dig up, one day" (94).

In a puritan society privacy is an important condition for retaining identity: the smallest bits of privacy can nurture the self's salvation and protect one's dignity. In Gilead private consciousness is all that is left; it cannot be regulated by the state. Offred may have lost most of the power to control others, to observe and control her world, but she still controls her private thoughts:

I used to think of my body as an instrument, of pleasure, or a means of trans-portation, or an implement for the accomplishment of my will. I could use it to run, push buttons, of one sort or another, make things happen. There were limits but my body was nevertheless lithe, single, solid, one with me.

Now the flesh arranges itself differently. I'm a cloud, congealed around a central object, the shape of a pear, which is hard and more real than I am and glows red within its transluscent wrapping. Inside it is a space, huge as the sky at night and dark and curved like that, though black-red rather than black.   (83–4)

In this drama of power and powerlessness, Atwood clearly shows that certain types of oppression ensnare the oppressor along with the oppressed – power is always ambiguous. One of the explanations for the peculiarly ambiguous position of the implied author is her commitment to an essentially *romance* novel genre: she cannot help dramatizing horror and rhetoricizing violence, and she cannot help but make her "heroine" into a figure of compelling existential fortitude. This is not a negative judgment of the novel but simply an unveiling of its rhetoric's origins and intentions. Atwood has an ethical imperative, but she also has an rhetorical one – to create a convincing and suspenseful story. It is, of course, paradoxical that without imagining the dystopic situation, a conditional future of male tyranny, the implied author would not have a stage upon which to dramatize Offred's integrity.

I am suggesting that Atwood is experimenting with the deployment of compelling rhetorical form and with the rhetorical attraction of special conflicts. Take away the danger and repressiveness of Gilead – its Eyes, its Guardians, and its hangings – and you no longer have the persuasive climate that justifies Offred's quietly strident discourse:

Maybe none of this is about control. Maybe it isn't really about who can own whom, who can do what to whom and get away with it, even as far as death.

Maybe it isn't about who can sit and who has to kneel or stand or lie down, legs spread open. Maybe it's about who can do what to whom and be forgiven for it. Never tell me it amounts to the same thing.   (144–5)

In *The Handmaid's Tale* we are guided by a cunning implied author, a voice that feigns weakness in the guise of Offred, her narrative mask; but this voice cannot help but advertise the control and strength of its origins: Margaret Atwood. The implied author plays a narrator who subjects her audience to a terrible nightmare in which she is the heroine. At one point she asks our forgiveness: "I'm sorry there is so much pain in this story. I'm sorry it's in fragments ... Because I'm telling you this story I will your existence. I tell, therefore you are" (279). But even this request is followed by a move that makes us conscious of the *writer's* power, for though this reader has participated and intervened in the critical reconstruction of this story, responsibility for its pain and power is shared with the rhetorical will of the author.

8 Conclusion

The innovative fictions that have been considered in this book present authority and power relations, and the problem of individual autonomy and fulfillment, as central themes: the attitudes towards these themes are often highly ambiguous. In *The Double Hook* the psychology of family conflicts, jealousy over election and social control, and the problem of reconciling conflicting interests in the community are central. In *Beautiful Losers* there is less interest in the problem of achieving unity than in dissolving oppressive uniformity and the mechanistic aspects of modern life through a psychic revolution that is allegorized through violence, declamatory rhetoric, and sexual experiment. In *The New Ancestors* ethnocentrism, tribalism, and colonial imperialism are the central problems in the social and political order. In *Burning Water* the metafictional criticism of a patriarchal narrative legacy, the fictions created by men glorifying the conquests of other men, implicitly target male power as a central problem; in *Badlands* the approach to patriarchy is both supportive and subversive. In *The Handmaid's Tale* male power and the control over reproductive rights are central issues.

What kinds of assumptions about human nature are implicit in these novels? Watson's narrator assumes that people can be governed by spiritual intuition and need the consolations of faith in the ineffable; Cohen's narrators assume that people are essentially repressed, overly rational, and need Dionysian release; Godfrey's, that people are essentially self-interested, are sometimes victims of socially imposed barriers, and that their rich internal lives are tragically inaccessible to their closest friends. Kroetsch's narrator assumes that sexual difference is central to understanding the human condition and that sexual power is essentially ambiguous and unpredictable; Bowering's, that human nature is not accessible to deliberate psychological analysis but that the most profound insights into people come accidentally, randomly. Atwood assumes that men and women are definable by the power relations between them, that they are perpetually trapped in tactics of self-preservation, in strategies of control, and in the pleasure that comes from the control of others.

Unlike Watson and Cohen, whose works urge the reader to accept an irrational view of social authority, Godfrey, Kroetsch, Bowering, and Atwood take up an explicitly critical attitude to social authority, and therefore they are the closest to claiming true counter-ideological status. But the critical attitude in these novels is complicated by the ambivalence of the implied authors towards their subject and towards their readers. This rhetorical ambivalence is reflected in Robert Kroetsch's *Badlands* in the tension between the feminist argument of the female narrator and the male sympathies of the omniscient implied author. Authorial ambivalence in Bowering's *Burning Water* is demonstrated by the writer's subscription to both "formalist" and "visionary" strategies of anti-referentiality; he implies that the subject of art is the artistic process itself and that the external world is a fictional construct. He employs a self-referential rhetoric that advertises playfulness and ideological disinterest; but the kinds of authority that preoccupy Bowering – evidenced by his interest in male competition, militancy, and pride – contradict his professions of ideological innocence. Margaret Atwood's *Handmaid's Tale* presents a feminist dystopia designed to show a subjugated narrator, but this character manifests an ambiguous attitude to the mechanisms of subjugation and control.

The attitudes to authority that are presented in all these novels are in some way ambivalent; they are all concerned with the contradictory desires that are evoked in the presence of authority. In Watson authority gives rise to both the irrational desire for rebellion and the desire for harmony through obedience; in Cohen it evokes a desire for liberation from oppressive social conventions as well as a desire for a loss of individual responsibility for control; in Godfrey it elicits a desire for individual autonomy and for tribal solidarity and community; in Kroetsch's narrator it compels the appropriation of the mechanisms of male authority and freedom as well as the desire to escape authority, to break free into a private female world where a new identity can flourish. In Bowering the authority of past history provokes a desire for Heraclitean freedom from predictability as well as a need for meaningful, even if accidental, connections to the past; in Atwood authority (male and female conservatism) compels the desire for liberation and yet it also provokes a fascination with the excitement of using power.

How is the authority of the author's ideology mobilized to elicit our "serious" reading? The six novels examined present a wide range of rhetorical procedures. The levels of discourse that each work contains range from the single narrator who establishes an authoritative, superior, and oblique footing and is aligned with the implied author in *The Double Hook* to the multiple voices that script intimate, equal, and confessional footings that elicit sympathy in *The New Ancestors*. The types of argument that these novels present are reflected in the types of footings they utilize to script the imaginary social relationship with the reader: the impersonal single voice is used for authoritative assertion in *The Double Hook*; the personal and confrontive voice is used for shocking personal catharsis in *Beautiful Losers*; the juxtaposition of contradictory points of view – impersonal and personal, confrontive and oblique, formal and informal footings – sets up arguments that depend on ironic comparison in *The New Ancestors, Badlands, Burning Water*, and *The Handmaid's Tale*.

In Watson, who dramatizes the power struggle between forces of individuality and community, there is the discourse of the "community" (the thoughts of characters) and the discourse of the prophet, who is always present to mediate the experiences of the community and who assumes epistemological primacy. In Cohen, who dramatizes the decadent pursuit of self-immolation, there is the rhetoric of the master, who orchestrates the wild linguistic orgies, and that of the slave: Cohen's narrators simultaneously exert mastery over the reader – by inundating us with copious sexual hallucination – and kneel before us as supplicating, powerless, frightened victims. In Godfrey, who attempts to dramatize both the liberal concern for the individual and the Marxist's interest in social constraints, there are narrative strategies that correspond to liberal and Marxist orientations to character: stream of consciousness and objective narration. In Kroetsch, who dramatizes the struggle between male public power and the female need for personal identity, there are two types of voice: a third-person omniscient voice sympathetic to the public world of the male, and a first-person female voice that is self-reflexive and critical of male being. In Bowering, who dramatizes both his comically random "research" of Vancouver and the captain's careful charting of the sea, there is third-person "objective" narration of Vancouver and first-person self-conscious authorial address. In Atwood, who dramatizes the desire for liberation and the fascination of control, there is the paradox of a narrator who is characterized as ingenuous yet who has tremendous narrative skill.

What useful conclusions can be drawn from the varieties of narrative strategies and effects, from such an array of positionings of readers and authors in terms of "power"? There are inherent contradictions in the liberating attitudes of all texts, a contradiction that is part of the dissemination of any knowledge: writers (parents, teachers, critics) attempt to "liberate," enlighten, free, and make more independent their "readers" (children, pupils); but this liberation process can be seen as inherently contradictory because of the constraints that the discourse imposes on the receiver. As Michel Foucault writes, "Power must be analysed as something which circulates, or rather as something which only functions in the form of a chain. It is never localised here or there, never in anybody's hands, never appropriated as a commodity or piece of wealth. Power is employed and exercised through a net-like organisation. And not only do individuals circulate between its threads; they are always in the position of simultaneously undergoing and exercising this power" (*Power* 98). The dissemination of any knowledge is contradictory because it involves both power transfer and reinscription of a new bond of inequality between the wielder of the discourse and the addressee. According to these texts, readers are both slaves to and masters of the text.

The relationship between a novel's propositions concerning authority and its form is not simply complementary. There are varying degrees of tension, ambivalence, and sometimes contradiction in the relationship between various narrators' uses of rhetoric and their professed beliefs concerning authority. Watson's *The Double Hook* promotes epistemological uncertainty, though the narrator speaks from a position of certainty. Cohen's narrators criticize cultural imperialism, though they decadently embrace defeat and enslavement. Godfrey tries to show the full range of a character's life, yet he does not treat all of them equally and he caricatures some characters from a clearly evaluative perspective. Narrators in Bowering, Kroetsch, and Atwood contradict their ideology by using forms of discourse that conflict with their implied political and metaphysical assumptions. The narrators here partly conceal their narrative power by foregrounding their ingenuousness or by attempting to conceal their positional advantage over the reader: Watson's narrator does not attempt to draw the reader's attention to her own omniscient position but quietly guides the reader with an unswerving hand; Bowering's narrator tries hard to convince the reader that he is an artless, playful rogue with no historiographic pretensions, yet his treatment of

Vancouver implies a counter-ideological motive; Atwood presents a narrator who is seemingly helpless, yet who is assigned narrative powers that skilfully place the reader in the realm of Gothic horror; even Kroetsch's narrators attempt to lull the reader into accepting the illusion of transparent mediation in those sections where they are impersonal and omniscient.

In drawing this rhetorical foray into the Canadian critical parlour to a close I am very conscious of the way that a method of reading has controlled some of the conclusions reached. The rhetorical criticism that I have used to examine the interplay of ideology and authority is interested, biased, and predisposed to discern and interpret a limited number of idioms, themes, categories, and formal textual phenomena. The method has proceeded in a predetermined contentious way to show contradictions; it has taken on a life of its own, following the inevitable tensions it scripts between warring themes, textual stances, and narrative poses (even here I am aware of the ironic rhetorical figuring of my method as an autonomous personality or a machine). However, all interpretation is similarly characterized by these conditions. Interpretation does not objectively recover some ideal or essential textual meaning but argues for the use of that text and is guided by procedures that are always conventional, procedures that work with and against a heritage of readings, citations, and intertexual traces; interpretation tells a story about the way that texts could be experienced from the point of view of a particular reader who is employing an implicit or explicit theory of textual reception.

Still, a question arises concerning the motives for rhetorical criticism. Why undertake this particular specialized form of criticism? One answer takes us back to the model of Burke's unending conversation in the critical parlour offered in the introduction to this book. Another answer takes us to the proprietary ways that critics regulate the readings of texts through model criticisms and the teaching of criticism in our institutes of education. Such resistant and contestatory criticism as I offer in this book will hopefully be useful and enabling for many readers: I think of the long rows of students in classrooms who may once have been transformed into the passive consumers of texts, who were not given an opportunity to challenge and resist the literature that they read because of the instructor's focus on a submissive and praising mode of reading. Texts have sometimes been treated as unanswerable authorities. This is not to say that such a sympathetic and receptive way of reading is unnecessary at an initial level. Such sympathetic reading is necessary and useful but it is not the only way to read, nor is it the best way to allow student readers to begin participating in the cultural conversations that surround them. Our questions should not always be the ones that assume or compel assent – "Isn't this work a fine realization of the quest structure?" – but should include questions that allow dissent as well – "What do you find acceptable or unacceptable about the point of view concerning the quest structure that is offered here? Is the implied author trying to get you to accept certain ideas in a way that you disagree with? Do you agree with this author's position as constructed by this particular critic?"

Innovative literary texts offer sites where we can sharpen our thinking about fundamental aspects of culture and ways of being, where we can try on roles, where the resistant reading can help us to become more than mere consumers of beliefs, indeed active producers of texts ourselves. This does not mean that we need to play the same resistant interpretive role each time, or that others trying to play the role as the kind of reader I have constructed for this book will come to the same conclusions. As George Dillon puts it, "It is not our own true selves that we bring to reading and enact there. At most it is a version, one role among several that we might play as we read, though it might be the serious role of earnestness, innocence, and submissiveness" (*Rhetoric as Social Imagination* 148).

We should also emphasize that writers also play several roles in their writing. It is not their true selves that they bring into the writing, but one role among many. It should not be assumed that the "real" authors are simply connected to the implied authors or narrators they construct: I must emphasize that in fact the "real" Sheila Watson, Leonard Cohen, David Godfrey, Robert Kroetsch, George Bowering, or Margaret Atwood does not resemble the implied authors of his or her texts; the real voices of these authors are not accessible to us. Despite what Roger Fowler has said about the relevance of biographical contexts, we should recognize that biography is a conventional, constructed public text too, and that writers are presenting necessary public selves when they supplement the critical conversation with their own life and views; they have the right to disclaim the connection between their real selves and their narrative voices, or to suppress or even confound the connections.

Do I value the texts that are rhetoricized here? That our activity as buyers, readers, and critics of these postmodern texts legitimizes their uses of paradox, duplicity, and contradiction is noted by Linda Hutcheon writing in *The Politics of Postmodernism*: "Postmodernism paradoxically manages to legitimize culture (high and mass) even as it subverts it ... As producers or receivers of postmodern art, we are all implicated in the legitimization of our culture. Postmodern art openly investigates the critical possibilities open to art, without denying that its critique is inevitably in the name of its own contradictory ideology" (15). I recognize that I am also in this study showing the legitimacy of these works for serious rhetorical study: my critical conversation would not be possible without them; they exceed in their signification any totalizing control of anyone's exegesis. I respect these texts, seeing them as ingeniously made, important, and groundbreaking; but I have purposely not read them submissively. By taking these texts into the rhetorical seat of the critical parlour, I am in fact selecting them for special attention, implying they are significant enough for us to discuss, to analyse their importance, and strong enough to withstand the intervention. By drawing attention to them I hope that I am helping to legitimize them even though I am intervening into orthodox and compliant readings.

Intervention is something that all interpretation partakes of: the rhetoric of a text responds to the rhetorics of past influence; criticism supplements that rhetoric with further rhetoric. This means, as Stephen Mailloux cogently argues in *Rhetorical Power*, that interpretation always involves taking a position, a point of view, an evaluative perspective or footing: "To recognize the rhetorical politics of every interpretation is not to avoid taking a position. Taking a position, making an interpretation, cannot be avoided ... We are always arguing at particular moments in specific places to certain audiences ... If no foundationalist theory will resolve disagreements over poems or treaties, we must always argue our cases. In fact that is all we can ever do" (180–1).

I have tried to show that the analyses here are interested, that I am looking for the rhetorical power-plays in these texts, texts that are part of the contemporary power paradoxes of postmodernism. The texts of this study are ambivalent about power and control, and so is their rhetoric. They affirm and subvert the status quo. My reading of these texts also both affirms and subverts their cogency as suasive texts – for I have been both the controller and the controlled in this intervention. I also hope that these will not be the last words in this conversation and that you, the reader, will already have been enabled in arguing your own case as you have been reading.

Works Cited

Anderson, Bern. *The Life and Voyages of Captain George Vancouver*. Toronto: University of Toronto Press 1966.

Aristotle. *The Rhetoric and Poetics of Aristotle*. Trans. W. Rhys Roberts, intro. Edward Corbett. New York: Modern Library 1984.

Atwood, Margaret. *Survival*. Toronto: House of Anansi Press 1972.

– *Lady Oracle*. 1976. Toronto: Seal Books 1980.

– *The Handmaid's Tale*. Toronto: McClelland and Stewart 1985.

– *Cat's Eye*. 1988. Toronto: Seal Books 1989.

Auerbach, Erich. *Mimesis*. Trans. William Trask. 1953; New York: Anchor Doubleday 1957.

Bakhtin, Mikhail. *Rabelais and His World*. Trans. Helene Iswolsky. Cambridge: MIT Press 1968.

Banerjee, Chinmoy. "Alice in Disneyland: Criticism as Commodity in *The Handmaid's Tale*." *Essays on Canadian Writing* 41 (1990): 74–92.

Bartholomae, David, and Anthony Petrosky, eds. *Ways of Reading*. 2nd ed. Boston: Bedford Books 1990.

Bergmann, Harriet F. "Teaching Them To Read': A Fishing Expedition in *The Handmaid's Tale*." *College English* 51 (1989): 847–54.

Bloom, Harold. *The Anxiety of Influence*. New York: Oxford University Press 1973.

Booth, Wayne. *The Rhetoric of Fiction*. Chicago: University of Chicago Press 1961.

– *Critical Understanding*. Chicago: U of Chicago Press, 1979.

– *The Company We Keep*. Berkeley: University of California Press 1988.

Bowering, George. *Burning Water*. Toronto: General 1980.

– ed. *Fiction of Contemporary Canada*. Toronto: Coach House 1980.

- *The Mask in Place*. Winnipeg: Turnstone Press 1982.
- ed. *Sheila Watson and The Double Hook*. Ottawa: Golden Dog Press 1985.
- *Caprice*. 1987; Markham: Penguin 1988.
- *Harry's Fragments*. Toronto: Coach House 1990.

Bradbury, Malcolm, ed. *The Novel Today*. Glasgow: Fontana 1982.

Burke, Kenneth. *A Grammar of Motives*. New York: Prentice-Hall 1952.
- *A Rhetoric of Motives*. Berkeley: University of California Press 1969.
- *The Philosophy of Literary Form*. Berkeley: University of California Press 1973.

Cluett, Robert. "Surface Structures: The Synactic Profile of *Surfacing*." In *Margaret Atwood: Language, Text and System*, ed. Sherrill Grace and Lorraine Weir. Vancouver: University of British Columbia Press 1983. 67–90.

Cohen, Leonard. *Beautiful Losers*. 1966; New York: Bantam Books 1967.

Davey, Frank. *From There to Here*. Erin, Ont.: Press Porcepic 1974.
- *Surviving the Paraphrase*. Winnipeg: Turnstone 1983.
- *Margaret Atwood: A Feminist Poetics*. Vancouver: Talonbooks 1984.
- *Reading Canadian Reading*. Winnipeg: Turnstone 1988.

Davidson, E. Arnold. "Future Tense: Making History in *The Handmaid's Tale*." In *Margaret Atwood: Vision and Forms*, ed. Kathryn VanSpanckeren and Jan Garden Castro. Carbondale: Southern Illinois University Press 1988. 113–21.

Dillon, George. *Rhetoric as Social Imagination*. Bloomington: Indiana University Press 1986.

Eagleton, Terry. *Criticism and Ideology*. London: Verso Editions 1982.

Federman, Raymond, ed. *Surfiction*. Chicago: Swallow Press 1975.

Foucault, Michel. "What Is an Author?" In Harari, ed., *Textual Strategies*, 141–160.
- *Power/Knowledge*. Ed. Colin Gordon. New York: Pantheon 1980.

Fowler, Roger. *Linguistics and the Novel*. London: Methuen and Co. 1977.
- *Literature as Social Discourse*. London: Batsford Academic and Educational 1981.

Freeman, Donald, ed. *Linguistics and Literary Style*. New York: Holt, Rinehart, and Winston 1970.

Freibert, Lucy M. "Control and Creativity: The Politics of Risk in Margaret Atwood's *The Handmaid's Tale*." In *Critical Essays on Margaret Atwood*, ed. Judith McCombs. Boston: Hall 1988. 280–91.

Freud, Sigmund. *Civilization and Its Discontents*. New York: W.W. Norton and Company 1961.

Fromm, Erich. *Escape from Freedom*. New York: Avon Books 1965.

Garrett-Petts, W.F. "Reading, Writing, and the Postmodern Condition: Interpreting Margaret Atwood's *The Handmaid's Tale*." *Open Letter* 7, no. 1 (1988): 74–92.

Godard, Barbara. "'Between One Cliché and Another': Language in *The Double Hook*." In Bowering, *Sheila Watson*, 159–76.

Godfrey, Dave. *The New Ancestors*. Toronto: New Press 1970.

Graff, Gerald. *Literature against Itself*. Chicago: University of Chicago Press 1979.

– "The Pseudo-Politics of Interpretation." In Mitchell, *Politics of Interpretation*, 145–58.

Halliday, M.A.K. *Language as Social Semiotic*. London: Edward Arnold 1984.

Harari, Josué, ed. *Textual Strategies*. Ithaca: Cornell University Press 1979.

Hart, Roderick. *Modern Rhetorical Criticism*. Glenview, Ill.: Scott, Foresman 1990.

Harvey, Connie. "Tear Glazed Vision of Laughter." *Essays on Canadian Writing*, no. 11 (Summer 1978): 28–54.

Howe, Irving. *Politics and the Novel*. New York: Horizon Press 1957.

– *Decline of the New*. New York: Harcourt, Brace and World 1970.

– *The Critical Point*. New York: Horizon Press 1973.

Hutcheon, Linda. *Narcissistic Narrative*. New York: Methuen 1984.

– "Canadian Historiographic Metafiction." *Essays on Canadian Writing*, no. 30 (Winter 1984–85): 228–38.

– *The Canadian Postmodern*. Toronto: Oxford University Press 1988.

– *The Politics of Postmodernism*. New York: Routledge 1989.

Jameson, Fredric. "Postmodernism and the Consumer Society." In Kaplan, *Postmodernism*, 13–29.

Kaplan, E. Ann. *Postmodernism and Its Discontents*. London: Verso 1988.

Kilpatrick, William. *Identity and Intimacy*. New York: Dell Publishing Co. 1975.

Klinkowitz, Jerome. *Literary Disruptions*. Urbana: University of Illinois Press 1975.

Kreisel, Henry. "Sheila Watson in Edmonton." In Bowering, *Sheila Watson*, 7–8.

Kroetsch, Robert. *The Studhorse Man*. 1970; Toronto: Random House 1990.

– *Badlands*. Don Mills: General Publishing Co. 1975.

– *Labyrinths of Voice*. Edmonton: NeWest Press 1982.

– *Essays*. Open Letter, ser. 5 no. 4 (Spring 1983).

Kroker, Arthur. *Technology and the Canadian Mind*. Montreal: New World Perspectives 1984.

Kuehl, John. *Alternate Worlds: A Study of Postmodern Antirealistic American Fiction*. New York: New York University Press 1989.

Lacombe, Michele. "The Writing on the Wall: Amputated Speech in Margaret Atwood's *The Handmaid's Tale*." *Wascana Review* 21, no. 2 (1986): 3–20.

Lanham, Richard. *Style: An Anti-Textbook*. New Haven: Yale University Press 1977.

Lecker, Robert. "Freed from Story: Narrative Tactics in *Badlands*." *Essays on Canadian Writing*, no. 30 (Winter 1984–85): 160–86.

Leith, Dick, and George Myerson. *The Power of Address: Explorations in Rhetoric*. London: Routledge 1989.

Lennox, John. "The Past: Themes and Symbols of Confrontation in *The Double Hook* and 'Le Torrent.'" In Bowering, *Sheila Watson*, 47–61.

Lentricchia, Frank, and Thomas McLaughlin. *Critical Terms for Literary Study*. Chicago: University of Chicago Press 1990.

Lodge, David. *The Novelist at the Crossroads*. Ithaca: Cornell University Press 1971.

Lukács, Georg. *The Meaning of Contemporary Realism*. London: Merlin Press 1979.

Lyons, J., ed. *New Horizons in Linguistics*. London: Penguin 1970.

MacDonald, Larry. "Psychologism and the Philosophy of Progress: The Recent Fiction of MacLennan, Davies and Atwood." *Studies in Canadian Literature* 9 (1984): 121–43.

McHale, Brian. *Postmodernist Fiction*. New York: Methuen 1987.

MacKendrick, Louis K. "Robert Kroetsch and the Modern Canadian Novel of Exhaustion." *Essays on Canadian Writing*, no. 11 (Summer 1978): 10–27.

Mailloux, Stephen. *Rhetorical Power*. Ithaca: Cornell University Press 1989.

Malak, Amin. "Margaret Atwood's *The Handmaid's Tale* and the Dystopian Tradition." *Canadian Literature* 112 (1987): 9–16.

Mandel, Ann. "Uninventing Structures: Cultural Criticism and the Novels of Robert Kroetsch." *Open Letter*, ser. 3, no. 8 (Spring 1978): 52–71.

Mandel, Eli. *Another Time*. Erin: Press Porcepic 1977.

– ed. *Contexts of Canadian Criticism*. Toronto: University of Toronto Press 1977.

Marcuse, Herbert. *The Aesthetic Dimension*. Boston: Beacon Press 1978.

Margeson, Robert. "A Preliminary Interpretation of *The New Ancestors*." *Journal of Canadian Fiction* 4, no. 1 (1975): 96–110.

Mitchell, Beverly, S.S.A. "Association and Allusion in *The Double Hook*." In Bowering, *Sheila Watson*, 99–113.

Mitchell, W.J.T., ed. *The Politics of Interpretation*. Chicago: University of Chicago Press 1983.

Monkman, Leslie. "Coyote as Trickster in *The Double Hook*." In Bowering, *Sheila Watson*, 63–9.

Morriss, Margaret. "The Elements Transcended." In Bowering, *Sheila Watson*, 83–97.

Moss, John, ed. *Present Tense*. Toronto: NC Press 1985.

Newman, Charles. *The Post-Modern Aura: The Act of Fiction in an Age of Inflation*. Evanston: Northwestern University Press 1985.

Northey, Margot. "Symbolic Grotesque." In Bowering, *Sheila Watson*, 55–61.

Ondaatje, Michael. *Leonard Cohen*. Toronto: McClelland and Stewart 1970.

O'Neill, John. "Postmodernism and Post (Marxism)." In Silverman, *Postmodernism*, 69–79.

Ong, Walter. *Orality and Literacy*. London: Methuen and Co. 1982.

Orwell, George. *Nineteen Eighty-four*. 1949; Harmondsworth: Penguin Books 1984.

Pease, Donald. "Author." In Lentricchia, *Critical Terms*, 105–17.

Plato. *Gorgias*. Trans. W.C. Hembold. 1952; Indianapolis: Bobbs-Merrill 1979.

Poggioli, Renato. *The Theory of the Avant-Garde*. Cambridge: Belknap Press 1968.

Rooke, Constance. "Interpreting *The Handmaid's Tale*: Offred's Name and the 'Arnolfini Marriage.'" *Fear of the Open Heart: Essays on Contemporary Canadian Writing*. Toronto: Coach House 1989. 175–96.

Rubenstein, Roberta. "Nature and Nurture in Dystopia: *The Handmaid's Tale*." In *Margaret Atwood: Vision and Forms*, ed. Kathryn VanSpanckeren and Jan Garden Castro. Carbondale: Southern Illinois University Press 1988. 101–12.

Said, Edward. *Orientalism*. New York: Vintage Books 1978.

Scholes, Robert. *Fabulation and Metafiction*. Urbana: University of Illinois Press 1979.

Seim, Jeanette. "Horses and Houses: Further Readings in Kroetsch's *Badlands*." *Open Letter*, ser. 5, nos. 8–9 (Summer-Fall 1984): 99–115.

Sennett, Richard. *Authority*. New York: Alfred A. Knopf 1980.

Sharratt, Bernard. *Reading Relations: Structures of Literary Production*. Brighton: Harvester Press 1982.

Silverman, Hugh, ed. *Postmodernism*. New York: Routledge 1990.

Stevick, Philip. ed. *The Theory of the Novel*. New York: Free Press 1967.

– *Alternative Pleasures*. Urbana: University of Illinois Press 1981.

Suleiman, S., & I. Crosman, eds. *The Reader in the Text*. Princeton: Princeton University Press 1980.

Thomas, Peter. *Robert Kroetsch*. Vancouver: Douglas and MacIntyre 1980.

Vickers, Brian. *Classical Rhetoric in English Poetry*. 1970. Carbondale: Southern Illinois University Press 1989.

Watson, Sheila. *The Double Hook*. 1959; Toronto: McClelland and Stewart 1969.

Woodcock, George, ed. *The Canadian Novel in the Twentieth Century*. Toronto: McClelland and Stewart 1975.

Zamyatin, Yevgeny. *We*. Trans. Mirra Ginsburg. New York: Avon Books 1972.

Zola, Emile. *The Experimental Novel and Other Essays*. Trans. B. Sherman. New York: Haskell House 1964.

Index